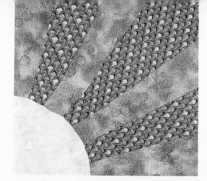

100 Traditional and Contemporary

Quilt Blocks

Celia Eddy

SEARCH PRESS

A QUARTO BOOK

Published in 2010 by Search Press Ltd.
Wellwood
North Farm Road
Tunbridge Wells
Kent
TN2 3DR

ISBN 978-1-84448-557-4

QUAR.QBB

Conceived, designed and produced by
Quarto Publishing plc
The Old Brewery
6 Blundell Street
London N7 9BH

Project Editor Kate Tuckett
Art Editor and Designer Julie Francis
Assistant Art Director Penny Cobb
Text Editors Jean Coppendale, Deirdre Clark
Illustrator Jennie Dooge
Photographer Martin Norris, Ian Howes
Indexer Pamela Ellis

Art Director Moira Clinch
Publisher Piers Spence

Manufactured by PICA Colour Separation Private Ltd.,
Singapore
Printed by Midas International Printing Ltd., China

Contents

Introduction

'Discovering Patchwork' was the title of a series of television programmes shown in the mid-1970s. I saw it by chance – and it changed my life. I became completely hooked on patchwork and quilting and have been ever since. I'm still exploring and learning – and I know I shall never come to the end of all the creative possibilities of this uniquely satisfying craft.

I've been fascinated by mosaic patterns since I was about five years of age, when I was given an old-fashioned kaleidoscope as a Christmas present. It was my best present ever and I spent many happy hours lost in that ever-changing world of colours and patterns that magically appears as you look through the peephole. When, as an adult, I discovered patchwork, it took me straight back to that childhood experience. It introduced me to an exciting new way of creating patterns but with the added thrill of applying skill rather than trusting to chance to make them. And there was also the bonus of being able to put the results to uses, which could be either practical or beautiful or perhaps both at the same time.

That's the great thing about patchwork: it allows you to combine the fun of designing and manipulating colours and shapes with the possibility of a practical and artistic application. One piece of patchwork might go on your bed to keep you warm on a cold winter's night. Another might be thrown over a

◄ *'Ohio Twist'*
bed quilt.
Machine pieced,
hand quilted.
Celia Eddy,
2001.

couch for your pets to snuggle down on. A third you might even wear, as a coat or a dress. Others you might hang as works of art, either on your own walls at home or on the walls of a gallery. And, best of all, absolutely anyone can do it!

The beauty of blocks

Blocks are the easiest, most user-friendly quilt-making medium. A big project such as a quilt for a double bed can seem quite a daunting task to begin with. But working in blocks breaks down the work into manageable units and, as each one is completed and laid aside, you soon start to get a real sense of achievement and feel encouraged to press on until you have as many as you need.

(A word of warning: if you're like me and often find yourself falling in love with a block and deciding you simply have to try it out, watch out or you may find yourself living in a house full of cushions, each a memorial to one of those 'block passions!')

The best reason of all for working in blocks is the wonderful secondary patterns that can appear when blocks are placed together. So, for each block illustrated in the Blocks section, I've shown at least one example of the beautiful effects that can be obtained by repeating the block.

It's so easy!

Sometimes people ask me if I know a lot about mathematics. They see that many patchwork blocks are based on complex geometry and, as a result, feel that patchworking is not for them.

▲ 'Star Octagon' wall quilt. Machine pieced, machine quilted. Celia Eddy, 2001.

▼ Cushion showing Barbara Fritchie block.

But, in fact, to make your own patchwork blocks you don't need to know a single thing about geometry, and you need never draft or draw a single pattern. Why? Because there are thousands of published patterns already available, often with full-size templates and patterns for you to use.

On the other hand, creating your own designs is great fun and very rewarding. One of the aims of this book is to give you the basic tools to get you started, if that's what you

▾ Streak o' Lightning (top) and Virginia Star (bottom) blocks

want to do. You'll learn how to interpret traditional blocks to create your own designs, how to invent your own blocks and how to manipulate fabrics and colours to achieve unique effects.

Some people are put off patchwork, not only by the geometry but also by the feeling that to do it you need to be expert with a sewing needle. In fact, the practical side of patchwork is as easy as the pattern-making. At its most basic, an ability to sew in running stitch, whether by hand or using a sewing machine, is all you need. All patchwork blocks are created from nothing more complicated than the sewing together of different shapes, even if some of them do need a little more care than others.

Although I've mainly focused on pieced blocks, appliqué also has been an important feature of block patchwork from very early times. A small selection of appliquéd blocks is therefore included so that you can learn the basics of this technique and try it for yourself.

Patchwork into quilts

Block patchwork is usually a means to an end – although I've mentioned that that end isn't necessarily a bed quilt. Whatever form you've decided your finished patchwork is going to take, you need to know how to complete it and present it. Although patchwork and quilting are two separate crafts, each with its own history, over time the two have become as closely associated as strawberries and cream, so you'll find details of how to make a complete patchwork quilt.

Of course, it is impossible to include here everything there is to know about either the art and craft or the history of patchwork and quilting. But what this book will do is give you all the information you need to make a wide variety of patchwork blocks and turn them into quilts. And it will also give you pointers towards detailed sources of information on any topic to help you find out more. My hope is that you'll want to know lots more about absolutely everything and that I'll have encouraged you to share my own fascination with this endlessly interesting activity.

▲ *Baltimore Style (top), Dresden Plate (middle), Oak Leaf and Cherries (bottom) blocks*

Celia Eddy .

The quilt block in history

The block is one of the oldest design resources known. What is believed to be the very oldest example of printed fabric is patterned with blocks. Look around you at familiar household items, and notice how many of them feature block designs.

▲ *Silk patchwork coverlet dated 1718, the earliest dated example of English patchwork.*

The block also has been around for a very long time in relation to quilt making. It was certainly a feature of English patchwork from early times. This has been proven by the earliest dated example, a silk coverlet dated 1718, measuring 274cm square (108 inches square) and worked entirely in 10cm (four-inch) blocks, including geometrical designs, human figures, plants, birds and animals.

But however long the pieced patchwork block may have been known in Europe, it was when it reached America that it really developed into an art form. European settlers took their own needlecraft skills and traditions with them across the Atlantic, but from them soon developed a uniquely American style and tradition.

American pieced blocks

It's hard for us today to imagine how isolated the pioneer settlers were. Previous experience was of only limited value in unknown territory and with limited and perhaps unfamiliar tools and equipment. So, solutions to problems had to be as simple as possible.

First, bedcovers were needed in large quantities and cloth was a valuable commodity so it made sense to salvage what was usable from worn-out items and other leftover scraps and then piece them into something new and useful. Second, piecing in blocks also had the advantage of being economical with both space and time.

Even today, block piecing carries nostalgic echoes of those tough pioneering days, when in their few spare moments hard-pressed women magically transformed their recycled fabrics into useful and beautiful quilts.

▾ *Medallion quilt echoing style of early English quilts.*

Almost all the earliest American quilts, from the seventeenth and eighteenth centuries, have perished. No doubt they were used and washed to death. But those few quilts that have survived from the last years of the eighteenth century are clearly related to European and particularly English styles of patchwork. As the nineteenth century progressed, piecing in blocks quickly became a lively – and distinctly American – tradition. In fact patchwork and quilting became forms of American folk art and craft. From that time until today, this work has been a continuous part of the social scene in America, particularly in rural areas, in a way that it never has been in Britain.

What's in a name?

In America, the collection and cataloguing of block names is a recognised field of study. There are several books on the subject containing lists of names and illustrations of blocks. Barbara Brackman's *Encyclopedia of Pieced Quilt Patterns*, for example, contains over 4,000 blocks and even that probably doesn't include every pattern that's ever been known and used.

Blocks are usually placed in categories according to the way in which they're drafted. (For more detail about those categories see pages 24–25.) Each of the most common categories is represented by several blocks. Many blocks have several alternative names. Here, the most commonly used names are given for the blocks illustrated together with a simple method for drafting each one.

New kids on the block

▼ *Log Cabin (top) and Kaleidoscope (bottom) blocks*

American magazines began publishing patterns for blocks as early as the 1830s, but those early patterns were mostly copies of English originals. By the 1880s, however, magazines were publishing completely new patterns, such as Fans and Log Cabins, which were seized on with enthusiasm by their readers. The patterns were almost exclusively pieced blocks, cotton fabrics were the materials of choice and the running stitch method of construction, known as 'American piecing', became the norm.

This was the time when the names given to blocks took on new importance. Many published patterns originated not with the magazines but with the magazines' readers, who submitted patterns for publication. Names given to these patterns might be personal to the designer, reflect current events or celebrate people and places. They might also be descriptive of what the pattern suggested to the eye, such as Kaleidoscope, Flying Geese, Lily or Pine Tree. While in 1907, *Hearth and Home* magazine requested designs for blocks named after states, capital cities and United States' territories. Before long, designs could be obtained by mail order, and by the 1920s even provincial newspapers began to carry patchwork and quilting columns.

A block by any other name...

Some blocks are known by many different names. In general, the more names a block has the older it's likely to be. To take just one example, the well-known North Carolina Lily appears in only slightly modified forms as Kentucky Lily, Mariposa Lily and Mississippi Pink. To add to the confusion, many blocks of unrelated design share the same name.

Block designs came from many sources. Some, such as Tumbling Blocks and Chevron, were based on geometrical figures, and they can be seen in antique floor tiles, wall mosaics and carpet patterns. Others are named for the natural objects and images which inspired them, such as trees, flowers, animals and features of the landscape. Ocean Waves, Storm at Sea and Stepping-Stones are examples of designs of that sort.

Many more blocks were named by their makers. Those names had personal meanings now tantalisingly lost. Who was the Sarah of Sarah's Choice, and who was Aunt Sukey? One thing's for sure, these ladies, whoever they were, would be amazed to know that their names still live on.

The names of many other blocks, such as Jacob's Ladder, Star of Bethlehem and Joseph's Coat had religious connotations. Particularly interesting are blocks that commemorate contemporary historical events. Examples include Whig's Defeat, Kansas Troubles and Yankee Pride.

Then and now

The invention of new blocks continues, which confirms that there's still plenty of life in this ancient design technique. What's more, by the time you've read this book, you'll be able to do just the same – create your own new blocks, invent your own names for them and so add your own stamp to the centuries-old chain of the quilt block tradition and heritage.

▲ North Carolina Lily (top), Storm at Sea (middle) and Jacob's Ladder (bottom) blocks

11

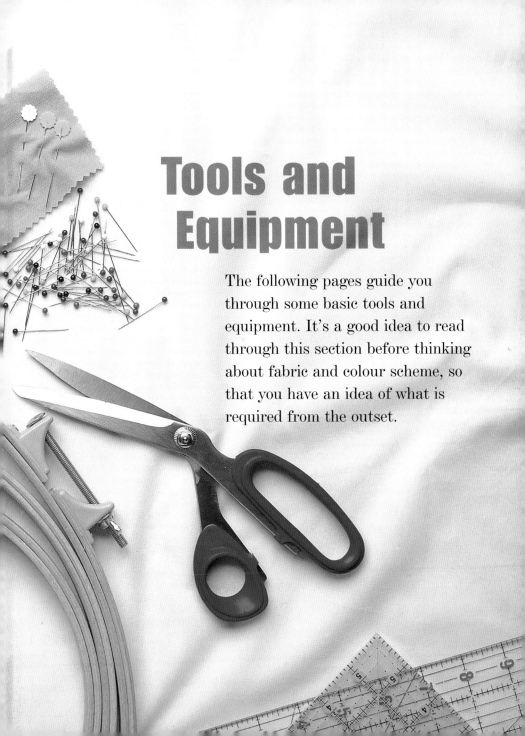

Tools and Equipment

The following pages guide you through some basic tools and equipment. It's a good idea to read through this section before thinking about fabric and colour scheme, so that you have an idea of what is required from the outset.

Tools and Equipment

All you really need to make patchwork are templates, scissors, fabric, needles and thread. To make a quilt, backing and wadding are added. Over the years, however, I've found the following to be useful additional items, from the many helpful products now available.

Unless you're copying printed templates, you need to be able to draft your own blocks.

❶ Graph paper Mostly, you'll be working on square grids, but isometric paper is invaluable for patterns based on triangles or hexagons.

❷ Cartridge paper Large sheets of drawing paper for drawing out full-size blocks.

❸ Pencils Some hard pencils for drawing accurate lines around templates. Softer ones can be used for marking quilts.

❹ Coloured pencils Watercolour pencils, crayons and felt-tip pens in a wide variety of colours and tones.

❺ Scissors Money spent at the outset on good-quality scissors is money well spent. You'll need:
- Scissors to be used only for cutting paper and templates.
- Fabric scissors. Large, heavy-duty scissors such as dress-making shears.
- Small, fine-pointed scissors for trimming.

❻ Template card or plastic
- Strong card needs to be cut with a small, sharp craft knife.
- A4 sheets of strong, clear plastic are easily cut with scissors.

❼ Rotary cutter and self-healing mat These have become standard equipment because they make cutting patches quickly so easy.

❽ Rulers You need rulers for drafting blocks and for measuring fabric. For drafting, choose a standard ruler. For fabric, there is a huge choice of special rulers. For use in cutting fabric on a self-healing mat buy one which is 15cm (6 inches) wide and as long as your mat is wide. Other useful sizes are a 30cm (12-inch) square which is ideal for drafting and squaring standard 30cm (12-inch) blocks, and a 60cm x 5cm (24 x 2-inch) ruler which is marked in millimetres.

❾ Tape-measure As well as an ordinary dressmaker's tape measure, a metal one is also useful for large quilts.

❿ Pins
- Glass-headed pins are easily seen.
- Flat-headed pins are useful for machine-quilting small projects as you can leave them in place while sewing.
- Ordinary dressmaking pins to use on patches.

⓫ Needles
- General-purpose sewing needles in a range of sizes for tacking and hand stitching.
- Special needles for hand quilting, called 'betweens', available in many sizes, ranging from 5, the thickest, to 12, which is very fine.
- General purpose sewing machine needles are fine for machine quilting and piecing.

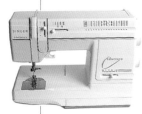

⓬ Sewing machine Although by no means an essential piece of equipment, many quilters today regard their sewing machine as their best friend. A basic model will be quite adequate for piecing patchwork, or computerised models are now available, some of which have special quilting functions. It's important to have a clear idea of what you want, however, and not go for one which has lots of unnecessary features. Useful features for a quilter are a swing-needle stitch and a reverse-stitch function enabling you to secure seams at the start and finish.

For piecing patchwork on the machine you need:
- A straight-stitch foot plate.
- A foot with a ½cm (¼-inch) guide to help keep an accurate seam allowance when sewing patches.

For quilting on the machine you will need:
- A walking, or even feed, foot.
- A darning foot.
- A means of covering or dropping the feed-dogs.

⓭ Fabrics
- Specialist cotton patchwork fabrics are ideal for washable bed-quilts. They come in a huge range of colours and patterns and are delightfully easy to sew and to quilt.
- Lining or backing fabric, which can be either patchwork cotton or other cheaper fabrics such as curtain lining. Remember, though, that if you want to hand-quilt it, avoid thick or dense-textured backing fabrics which will make it hard to push the needle through.

14 Wadding (US: 'batting') For the filling in the quilt 'sandwich', choose the right sort for your project. For bed quilts, a thicker wadding provides more loft, while for a wall quilt or garment, a thinner, closer-textured wadding might be used. Some waddings need closer quilting than others, so read the manufacturer's information to find out how much or how little quilting will be needed. This is important because wadding that is insufficiently quilted will tend to bunch up in the quilt and spoil it. The best plan is to get small pieces of different waddings and make samples to see how different ones behave, which may seem like a lot of trouble but will save you a lot of time and heartache later.

▾ Experiment with different waddings and establish which works best for you and your project.

The main types of wadding are:
- *Polyester* Although it is available in different weights, buy only good quality polyester wadding as the cheaper versions may cause 'bearding'. That is, the fibres migrate through the top layer and appear as a fine mist on the quilt surface, which looks particularly messy on dark fabrics. Some polyester waddings are needle-punched to prevent this from happening.
- *Cotton* Many versions are on the market, including some which are mixtures of cotton and made fibres.
- *Wool* Very soft and easily quilted.
- *Silk* A luxury item, but also beautifully soft and easy to quilt.

14

⑮ Thread

- Ordinary sewing threads, for hand and machine quilting. Make sure you only buy good quality threads, otherwise they'll break or snag in the sewing machine.
- Invisible threads, also called 'monofilament', are useful for machine quilting where you simply want to anchor the layers but don't necessarily want the stitches to show.
- Quilting threads are extra-strong, made to stand up to the stress of passing through the layers of a quilt. They come in a vast array of colours so you can match them to the colours of the fabric you are using, or choose contrasting threads for decorative effects.
- Embroidery threads and metallic threads have become very popular and are an easy way of embellishing your quilts. Special threads are available for decorative machine quilting, and it pays to ensure you get the correct ones for your sewing machine.

⑯ **Stitchripper** This little tool makes unpicking stitches without damaging the fabric easy, but it is also very handy for holding down small patches while you're stitching on the machine.

⑰ **Thimble** Even if you don't usually like to use a thimble, it's difficult to hand quilt without one. The best type of thimble for hand quilting has a small ridge around the crown, which prevents the needle from slipping. A finger guard is also useful for protecting the finger underneath the quilt.

⑱ Hoops and frames In order to quilt, the three layers of the quilt have to be held taut in a frame or hoop so that they don't slip apart while you're sewing. The most useful are:

- Floor-standing frames, either wood or plastic, for large quilts.
- Hoops for smaller items (illustrated).

⑲ Markers and erasers Traditionally, a variety of everyday household items would be used for marking patterns on quilts prior to quilting. These included slivers of soap and tailor's chalk and these can still be used. Other useful tools include:

- Soft pencils such as B.
- Vanishing marker pens, which make marks which can be washed out – only useful if you intend to wash your quilt before use.
- Special silver pencils for marking patterns on quilt-tops. The marks usually rub off easily.
- Chalk, which also rubs off easily.
- Fabric erasers for removing pencil marks.

⑳ For appliqué:

- Fusible webbing, which has adhesive on one side and paper on the other.

⑱

⑲

⑳

Choosing fabrics

Think about how your finished quilt is going to be used. For example, a bed quilt, intended for everyday wash-and-wear, is best made in a good quality cotton. Luckily, there is a vast range of cottons to choose from and, generally speaking, they're colourfast to light and water. However, you can never be certain that the colours won't run, so it's wise to wash. This is particularly important with dark fabrics. Patchwork cottons also have the added advantage of being easy to quilt.

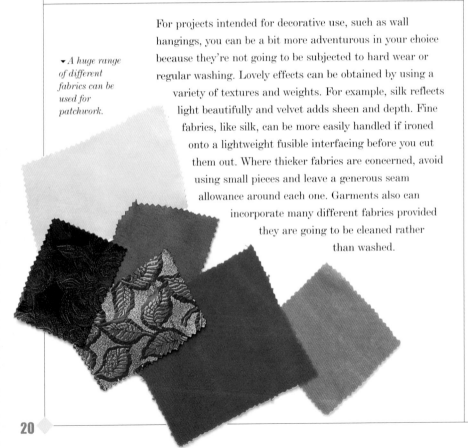

▾ A huge range of different fabrics can be used for patchwork.

For projects intended for decorative use, such as wall hangings, you can be a bit more adventurous in your choice because they're not going to be subjected to hard wear or regular washing. Lovely effects can be obtained by using a variety of textures and weights. For example, silk reflects light beautifully and velvet adds sheen and depth. Fine fabrics, like silk, can be more easily handled if ironed onto a lightweight fusible interfacing before you cut them out. Where thicker fabrics are concerned, avoid using small pieces and leave a generous seam allowance around each one. Garments also can incorporate many different fabrics provided they are going to be cleaned rather than washed.

How much fabric should you buy?

It's not difficult to estimate quantities for making small items, or even for a scrap quilt, but if you're planning a large quilt it's important to have some idea how much will be needed. One method is to make the templates for your block, cut out patches in either paper or scrap fabrics, then place them as economically as possible on some fabric that is the same width as that which you intend to buy – usually 114cm (45 inches). If you do this for each fabric you'll be using in the block, then add a generous allowance, at least 10 per cent to be safe, that will give you an idea of how much to buy. Alternatively, make up a single block and multiply the amount of each fabric used by the number of blocks you want to make.

For wadding and lining, measure the width by the length to get the size of pieces needed, then add at least 5cm (2 inches) all around because there will be some shrinkage during quilting.

▾ *Estimate the amounts of fabric you will need before buying the material.*

Working with colour and pattern

Colour theory is a fascinating subject; when it comes to quilt making, as with clothes or interior decorations, colour is a personal choice and it's difficult to lay down precise guidelines. We all have our favourite colours. But here are some general points that may be helpful.

Find a colour-wheel in a book, or make one for yourself by collecting a set of paintcards like those from home improvement stores. You'll find this invaluable when it comes to matching and comparing colours, and it will help you to identify the right fabric for your project.

Colours are often referred to as being in either the 'warm' range – reds, browns and purples – or the 'cool' range – blues and greens. Look at the colour-wheel and note which colours are grouped together and where the different ranges merge into each other. This knowledge can help to set the mood or style for your quilt.

When selecting colours, it's useful to recognise the difference between hue, value and intensity.

Hue Describes the position of a colour on the classic colour-wheel and names the colour: red, violet and green, for example.

Value Describes the lightness or darkness of the colour, that is its position on a scale from white to black.

Intensity Describes the depth, saturation and impact of the colour.

This knowledge will help you to achieve good contrasts, even within the same colour range, by varying these elements. Also, note that dark colours tend to advance towards the eye, while light ones retreat.

▲ *A simple colour-wheel shows the relationship between colours and is a useful design aid.*

Tip

You can get a good effect of distance by pinning fabrics to a cork board and looking at them through the wrong end of a pair of binoculars. Even better is to pin a piece of white fabric to a door or wall and pin your fabrics to that.

In any pieced block, the variations you can create by changing and re-arranging colours and tones are almost infinite. Perceptions of colours are affected by the colours that surround them. This can produce surprising results. For example, put a blue border around a scrap quilt comprised of many different colours, and the blues will stand out. Add a green border and the greens will appear.

Many manufacturers of patchwork cottons produce ranges of fabrics that are colour-coordinated and which may include plains, large and small prints, checks, stripes and so on. If you want to achieve a coherent look to your quilt, these fabrics can be a wonderful aid, and you can always supplement the range by adding some fabrics of your own choice.

Patterns such as stripes and checks offer many design possibilities, and thus, even the simplest block can have interesting visual impact. You can also use large patterns to create kaleidoscopic effects by placing a transparent template over the pattern elements you want to use, then positioning two mirrors so that the pattern is repeated. This shows you where to place the template.

▲ *Patterned fabrics can be used to enhance block designs.*

◄ *Kaleidoscope effect with mirrors.*

Drafting blocks and making templates

Instructions for blocks are traditionally given in imperial, but metric templates and rulers are now standard. Indeed, many items are marked in both imperial and metric units. Where measurements are given here, both units are provided.

Drafting blocks

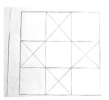

The blocks in this book have been drafted according to the grid system, which is traditionally used as a way of categorising blocks. Not all authorities agree on the exact categorisation of particular blocks, but I have identified twelve commonly recognised categories and placed each block accordingly. Each block is shown with a diagram of its construction. To draft any block, first draw a square of the size you want for your finished block on cartridge paper. Conventionally, pieced blocks are usually 30cm (12 inches) square when finished, but if you follow the method outlined below you can choose any size you like. Once you've drawn your block, you can have a lot of

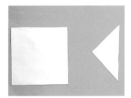

1 Draw a grid with the required number of lines. Draw in the construction lines.

2 To make templates, identify each of the shapes required and cut out each one. Stick your paper shape down either onto card or onto a plastic template.

3 Unlike English patchwork, templates for American patchwork include the seam allowance, usually ½cm (¼ inch), so carefully draw around the shape ½cm from the line and cut out.

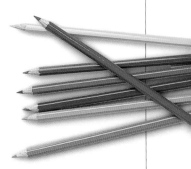

fun trying out different colour effects. If you have a computer design program for quilting this becomes very quick and easy, but you really don't need one. I spent years playing with blocks, using nothing more sophisticated than coloured pencils and a duplicator before quilt design programs were invented, and you can do the same. Here's how:

▲ *Quilt designs can either be drafted by hand or on a computer.*

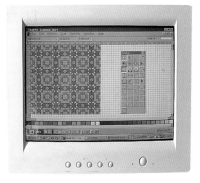

1 Draw your block and shade it. At this stage, it's best to use black, white and greys to get the best impression of contrasts and tones.

2 Photocopy the block several times and stick the copies down on a sheet of paper in whatever arrangement looks best.

3 To add colour, make a blank version of your quilt layout – showing only the construction lines – photocopy it and then use coloured pencils, crayons or felt-tip pens to apply colour. If you make several copies of the layout you can try out different colourways. Kid's play!

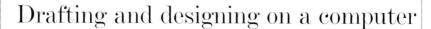

Drafting and designing on a computer

Computer-aided design (CAD) has become familiar to all sorts of designers, and it's no surprise that quilt makers have been quick to see the potential for their particular design interests.

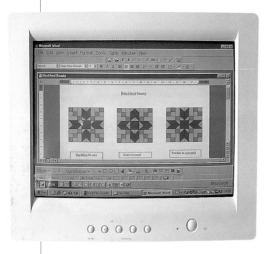

▲ *One block is manipulated into three designs here.*

There are several excellent programs now available specifically for quilt makers. They enable you to perform all the above design steps – but much more quickly. As well as helping you to draft and design your own blocks, they also contain ready-made 'libraries' of blocks for you to use. You can colour, rotate and flip them, then choose different borders and settings. There is usually a separate library of fabrics to try out, so you can get a really good idea of what your finished quilt will look like. In fact, just about every aspect of designing a block or a quilt can be dealt with, even down to the borders and sashings.

When you're happy with the design, you can print out templates to any size you like. This means you can try out a whole series of options before cutting out a single patch.

Of course, other graphics programs can also be used to design quilts and these offer more flexibility than the dedicated quilt design programs. Some design ideas using a quilt program are set out opposite.

Tumbling Blocks

Stars and Knots

Ohio Star set into Baby Blocks

Medallion (or Frame) quilt

Sewing blocks

This section introduces some of the different techniques used to construct patchwork blocks. It's definitely worth mastering more than one method as different blocks require different treatments.

American block piecing

Each block is made up of smaller pieces (patches) which are joined together, as shown in the diagram.

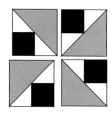

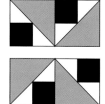

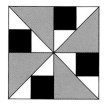

▲ *Steps in piecing a block*

Whether piecing by hand or machine, the process is the same. Patches are joined right sides together by a running-stitch seam, usually exactly ½cm (¼ inch) wide. The seams can be either pressed open or to one side, in which case try to press towards the darker of two fabrics to prevent the colour showing on the surface. It's important to press gently, putting the hot iron straight down onto the fabric. Avoid running the iron hard over the seams. If you prefer, you can finger-press each seam until the block is complete, then press it with the iron.

For hand sewing, some people find it helpful to use a ruler and pencil to mark each patch on the sewing line, ensuring that it's always an accurate ½cm (¼ inch) from the edge. Some sewing machines have a foot which clearly indicates ½cm (¼ inch) from the needle. The important thing is to sew an accurate ½cm (¼ inch) seam allowance or your patches won't fit neatly at the joins.

Set in seams   Most blocks can be constructed by sewing only straight seams. Occasionally, though, seams have to be 'set in', for example when sewing squares to diamonds to make box shapes. To do this, sew the first two patches together but without sewing into the seam allowance. Take a small backstitch at the end. You may find it easiest to make a dot on each patch to mark the allowance. Now join the third patch to the first one. Take a backstitch at the point where the two seams meet and secure the thread again. Pivot the third patch so that it lines up with the first patch and sew to the dot.

▲ *Setting in a patch*

Curved seams   Curved seams require careful sewing and it's worth trying out a few samples to learn the technique. The basic idea is to pin the curves so that you can ease the patches into shape. Cut notches in curves after stitching, then press. The Drunkard's Path is a good example of this.

Cutting out patches   Draw around each template on the fabric, using a soft B pencil, checking that the template includes a ½cm (¼ inch) seam allowance and add one if it doesn't. Cut out exactly on the line.

▲ *Pinning a curved seam*

Tip

When machine sewing, I usually mark a line on the plate so that I can see exactly where the edge of the fabric should be to ensure an accurate ½cm (¼ inch) seam allowance. Use a ruler with ½cm (¼ inch) markings. Place it under the needle exactly on the ½cm (¼ inch) line. Run a strip of masking tape on the plate along the edge of the ruler. Take a piece of cotton fabric, fold it in two and press the fold. Place the fold along the taped line and stitch a couple of inches. If the line of stitching isn't exactly ½cm (¼ inch) from the fold, repeat the process until it is. If you build up three or four layers of tape, it will create a ridge to keep the fabric on the line.

Using rotary cutter and mat To cut a lot of patches quickly and accurately, use a rotary cutter and mat. This will enable you to cut several layers of fabric together.

Of course, you can use the rotary cutting method to make accurate strips for borders and binding, cutting squares and many other shapes. Some commercially sold templates are made of strong, clear acrylic so you can safely cut round them with the rotary cutter for accurate patches.

1 First, you must trim the fabric: press the fabric with a hot iron then place it on the cutting mat with the rough, untrimmed side facing right. (Instructions here are for right-handed people. Reverse them if you are left-handed.) Place a ruler on the fabric, lining up the marking lines on the ruler so that it's at right angles to the fold in the fabric. Press down firmly on the ruler with your left hand and run the cutter smoothly along its edge.

2 Turn the fabric so that the trimmed edge is on the left. You can now cut strips of any width you wish by lining up the edge of the fabric with the markings on the ruler and cutting along the side of it. For cutting larger pieces, use the grid markings on the mat.

3 To make patches, measure the size of the template, and make strips of that width. Either cut around the template using the rotary cutter, or mark the shapes on the strip and then cut out using scissors.

English patchwork

Making patchwork by basting patches over templates then
oversewing patches together is traditionally called 'English',
or mosaic, patchwork. Its advantage is the ability to join
shapes with different angles accurately. An important
difference between English and American patchwork is that
the templates for English are exactly the size of the finished
patch – that is, they don't include a seam allowance.

1 Draw around your block
on cartridge paper and
identify the shapes you
need. For each shape,
make a master template
by sticking it down on
plastic or mounting board
and cutting it out. Trace
around it onto thick paper.

2 Cut out as many papers
of each shape as you'll
need for the block. Pin the
paper template to a piece
of fabric and cut it out
leaving a good seam
allowance round it. Baste
the fabric over the paper,
folding it exactly to the
edge of the paper. Go
round each side of the
patch, folding and mitring
the corners where
necessary.

3 Join two patches by
placing them face-to-face
and oversew the seam with
small stitches. Fit more
patches in the same way,
pivoting them to fit where
angles meet.

Tip
You can easily produce the same
effect for English patchwork
using the sewing machine. To do
this, you must still make the
patches as described. Place them
face-to-face and pin. Use
monofilament thread in the
spool of the machine and a
neutral colour in the bobbin, then
oversew the patches along each
seam using the zigzag function.

Foundation piecing

Foundation piecing is a useful technique for constructing blocks which require intricate piecing. It's particularly good for Log Cabin where the number of strips involved can often result in inaccurate measurements in the finished blocks.

You can work either on a very thin fabric foundation, such as fine muslin – in which case the foundation is left in the blocks – or on ordinary paper which will be torn off when the block is finished. The pattern of the block is marked on one side of the foundation. To make several blocks, either use a photocopier, or run copies off from a quilting program.

If you are using a paper foundation to be pulled off on completion, set your machine stitch shorter than usual, say 12 stitches to $2\frac{1}{2}$ cm (1 inch). Always take two or three stitches beyond the marked sewing line to secure it.

To sew Log Cabin blocks by this method, work from the centre of the block. Measure and cut each strip as you place it for stitching. Many other blocks can be constructed in this way but where lots of different shapes are required, the patches must be stitched in the correct order.

1 Place the centre square right side up on the UNMARKED side of the paper, making sure that it completely covers the stitching line – hold it up to the light to see this more clearly – and pin.

2 Take the first strip and place it over the centre square. Patch right sides together. Pin in position. Turn to the foundation paper and stitch along the marked line. Turn back to the right side and press the strip open.

3 Repeat this process until all the strips have been added. Now you can remove the papers, taking care not to pull too roughly on the stitches.

Appliqué

Appliqué is a way of making patterns by sewing contrasting fabrics onto a background. It's one of the oldest ways of decorating fabrics and has always been popular with quilt makers. It can be worked by hand or by machine.

Hand appliqué

1 For hand appliqué, draw or trace the shapes you want to apply and make templates of them. Draw around the templates on the fabric leaving a ½cm (¼ inch) allowance all round.

2 Press trimmings under, using the traced lines as guides. Baste all around. Pin to background fabric, and sew round the shape with small hemming stitches.

Machine appliqué

1 For machine appliqué, fusible webbing is the best method. Iron the webbing onto your appliqué fabric, taking care to place the webbing side face down. Then draw the required shape on the back of the webbing and cut out exactly to the line.

2 Peel off the paper and apply the shape to the background using a hot iron. Now use a small zigzag stitch to secure the shape all round.

Blocks into quilts

How many blocks do you need to make a quilt? Well, this is where you need to do some simple maths.

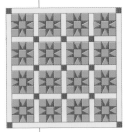

▲ *Sashings with posts*

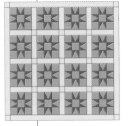

▲ *Plain sashings*

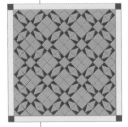

▲ *On point or diagonal setting*

Traditionally, blocks for bed quilts are 30cm (12 inches) square. Working on that scale, you'll need 24 blocks for a single bed quilt measuring 122cm x 183cm (48 inches x 72 inches) or 30 blocks for a bigger one measuring 153cm x 183 cm (60 inches x 72 inches). But there are other considerations, such as how wide your borders will be and if you're using sashings, which will be explained below.

Quilt layouts Lay the blocks out on a large surface – such as a bed. Move them around until you're happy with the layout. If you're thinking of adding sashings or borders, position some sample strips of fabrics that you might use and 'audition' different colours and patterns to get the best effect. Take care to keep the blocks in the correct order for sewing together in rows when you move them to the sewing machine. Pin and baste, as described, unless you're going to quilt in a frame.

There are several choices to be made when it comes to arranging your blocks for assembly into a quilt, some of which are illustrated here.

Possible settings include:

Straight set

On point or diagonal set

Alternate plain blocks

Plain sashings (interior borders)

Sashings with posts – in this case, the posts extend into the borders as well.

Adding borders

Plain borders

1 Measure your quilt from side to side and cut border strips of this length. Always measure in the middle of the quilt, not the sides, because small inaccuracies in the piecing may mean that the four sides aren't exactly the same in length. You can compensate for this by cutting the borders exactly to fit the centre measurement, then gently easing and adjusting the edges to fit.

Borders with corner posts

1 Measure the width of the quilt as before and cut two strips of this length.

2 Attach to top and bottom.

3 Measure the length of the quilt and cut two strips of this length.

4 Cut four squares in contrasting fabric with sides the same as the width of the border.

5 Add a square to each end of the two remaining border strips and attach to sides of quilt.

2 Attach top and bottom borders and press open. Measure again to find the length of the sides and cut two border strips of this length and attach them as before.

Borders with mitred corners (joined with a diagonal seam)

1 Measure the length and width of quilt.

2 Cut border strips of the same measurements, but add twice the width of the border to each one.

3 Add borders to all sides but stitch only to within ½cm (¼ inch) of the end of the seam on all sides.

4 Press the borders open and lay the quilt out on a flat surface. Lap one strip over another at the corners.

5 Fold the top strip under at an angle of exactly 45 degrees and pin carefully.

6 Slip stitch the top to the bottom and trim excess.

Adding sashings   I find it useful to make a quick sketch of the layout of the quilt on squared paper so I can work out how many strips – and squares where applicable – I need.

Plain sashings

1 Decide on the width of the sashings – usually the same width as the borders. Work out how many strips you need and cut out the required number. If your blocks measure 30cm (12 inches), cut the strips the same length.

2 Join the blocks in rows by adding a strip to the first block, then joining the second block to it and so on.

3 Measure the rows, cut sashing strips of that length and join the rows. Add borders as described on page 35.

Sashings with posts

1 Work out how many strips and squares are needed for the number of blocks you've got.

2 Cut the strips to fit the blocks and attach as in step 3 above.

3 Cut squares with sides the same as the width of the strips.

4 Join the squares and sashing strips.

5 Join the rows, taking care to match up the seams at each join.

Assembly

1 Lay out the quilt backing fabric the WRONG side up, on a large, flat surface – you may have to resort to the floor for this if it's a big quilt. The backing and wadding should be at least 4cm (1½ inches) bigger all round than your quilt top. Stretch it out and smooth it to remove any wrinkles or creases.

2 Lay the wadding over the backing.

3 Finally, lay the quilt top on the wadding. Depending on whether you're going to quilt by hand or by machine, proceed as described below for each method.

Quilting Quilting is simply a way of anchoring three layers of fabric together . You can choose from several methods:

'In the ditch' The quilting stitches are worked exactly along the seam lines, and are invisible.

Outline quilting The quilting stitches are worked around the patches, usually ½cm (¼ inch) away from the patch.

Echo quilting Several rows of quilting stitches follow the outline of shapes on the quilt surface.

Whole cloth quilting Plain blocks, or even a whole quilt, are quilted with decorative patterns.

Stipple quilting A hand quilting, infill technique for covering areas with tiny, randomly placed stitches.

Trapunto Shapes are outlined by quilting stitches, then padded with small pieces of batting inserted from the back.

Tied A quilt sandwich is anchored by passing a thread through the layers, bringing it to the surface and tying off.

Preparing to hand quilt in a frame To hand quilt on a large frame, set the quilt sandwich into the frame. One end of the quilt is pinned or tacked to one of the 'rollers' then rolled round until only a small portion is left. To get the correct tension, tapes are attached to the sides of the quilt and secured on the 'stretchers'. This way, you don't need to baste before you begin quilting.

Preparing to hand quilt in a hoop First pin through all three layers over the whole quilt to prevent them sliding apart. The next stage, basting, is the key to easy and successful quilting. Use a long needle and tailor's tacks. Keep the layers as taut as possible. Basting can either be done in straight lines in a grid across the quilt or diagonally. Place your portion of the quilt in the hoop: the tension should be slack enough to enable you to manoeuvre the needle through the layers easily and smoothly.

▲ *Outline quilting*

▲ *Tied quilting*

▲ *Trapunto quilting*

Tip
If, like me, you've got a floor-standing frame but sometimes prefer to quilt in a hoop, it's worth placing the quilt in the frame while you baste it. Then take it out and use the hoop as described.

▲ *Hand quilting*

▲ *Machine quilting*

Hand quilting Wearing a thimble, use strong quilting thread and a quilting between needle (see page 15). For a beginner, a size 10 needle is about right. Make a knot in the end of the thread. Bring the needle up from the back of the quilt and gently pull the knot through into the wadding. Then take a small backstitch and begin to quilt. The aim is for every stitch to pass through all three layers of the quilt. You'll find it easier to do this by keeping the needle as upright as possible using the thimble to push it through. With your other hand under the place where you're quilting, feel the needle point as it comes through. Now pick up about four stitches on the needle before pulling it back up. At the end of the thread, take another small back stitch through all the layers, run the thread back through the wadding for a couple of centimetres and cut off.

Machine quilting Prepare for machine quilting as described for hand quilting, by basting the quilt all over. There are two main methods for machine quilting, one for straight-line quilting, and the other for 'free' designs. If you're a beginner, it's best to stick to straight-line quilting until you've learned the techniques.

Straight-line quilting Either mark the lines on the quilt surface with chalk or pencil, or use the edge of the pressure foot to make evenly spaced lines of stitching.
- Attach a walking or even-feed foot that prevents the layers from moving apart as you stitch.
- Adjust the tension to being looser than for normal sewing.
- Roll the quilt up to leave just enough free to work on.
- Start and end with a couple of reverse stitches.
- At the end of each section, thread the loose ends into a needle, pass through the layers and snip off at the back.

Tip
Instead of marking straight lines, I lay strips of masking tape of the required width on the surface and use them as a stitching guide.

Free quilting Ideally you should be able to adjust your machine to a level so that you can move the quilt around freely. You can either place the section to be quilted in a hoop or hold it in position.

- Cover the feed-plate and attach a darning foot.
- Adjust the stitch length to 0; reduce the tension slightly.
- Run the machine at a slower rate than for normal sewing.
- Move the quilt to make the needle follow the pattern.
- Secure and snip the threads as described above.

Finishing the quilt You can finish the edges by one of the following methods:

Binding

5 Fold over to the back and neatly slip stitch them to the backing without letting the stitches show through on the surface.

6 Measure again and add side strips in the same way. Allow extra length on the binding for the sides to turn in at the corners.

1 Lay the quilt on a flat surface and trim evenly all round.

2 Measure the width in the middle of the quilt and cut strips of 6cm (2½ inches) wide fabric to match.

3 Fold the strips double and press with a hot iron.

4 Pin to the edges of the quilt at the top and bottom.

Butting

1 Lay the quilt on a flat surface and trim as before.

2 Turn the quilt top over the wadding then turn the backing onto it.

3 Slip stitch the sides together.

Backing fabric to front This is an alternative way to finish. Simply fold the backing over to the front and hem it to the surface of the quilt.

The Final Touch! Always add a label to your quilt with your name, the date and perhaps a dedication if the quilt is intended as a gift.

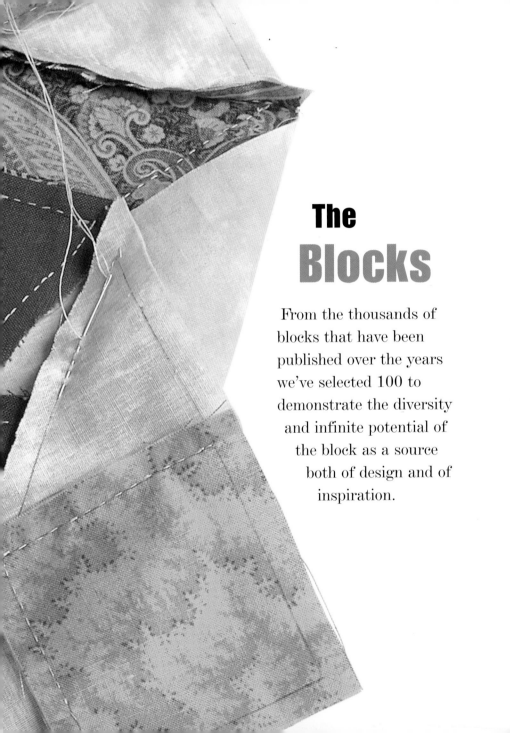

The
Blocks

From the thousands of
blocks that have been
published over the years
we've selected 100 to
demonstrate the diversity
and infinite potential of
the block as a source
both of design and of
inspiration.

How to use this book

This book will help you to learn all the basic skills involved in drafting and making blocks and turning them into quilts. And that's just the beginning of the story, because you can go on to make up your own blocks and design your own quilts with them, as I'll explain in Where to go from here.

The introductory material has already dealt with straightforward instructions on all the processes involved, from drafting the blocks and making templates, through to piecing blocks and turning them into quilts. Using this as a guide, you'll be able to make any of the blocks in the book.

You'll see that each block is graded according to difficulty using the ✎ symbol. Of course, even as a beginner you may be excited by a particular block which is more difficult to construct, in which case, once you've made the templates, you can simplify matters by hand-piecing, following the instructions on page 28.

Geometrical blocks are traditionally categorised according to the underlying grid on which they are drafted. Once you've grasped this idea you can draft almost any block you come across, whether in a quilt, a magazine or a book. Most of the blocks in the twelve categories here can be constructed on grids. Blocks with curved patches almost always need to be drafted with a protractor but if you find this daunting, or don't want to go to the trouble, simply photocopy the pattern and enlarge it to the size you want. The same is true of the fan blocks and of appliqué blocks, although some of these can also be drafted on grids.

Your first decision in any patchwork and quilting project is, of course, what you're going to make! How many blocks do you need to make? Which layout will you use? For example, if you intend to make a bed-quilt, you may decide to use a fairly simple block or to alternate pieced and plain blocks. Look back at the basic instructions for suggestions.

When you feel confident you've got the basic ideas and methods, there are lots of other ideas and suggestions in the Where to go from here section.

The small top left artwork represents the block multiplied. Sometimes a variation is also shown, in which case a short explanatory caption is added.

denotes an easy project; is more advanced.

The single block shown here is sometimes displayed with a border as a finished work in itself.

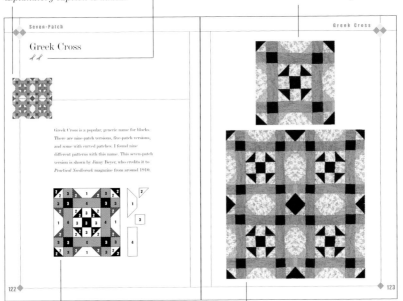

Seven-Patch

Greek Cross

Greek Cross is a popular, generic name for blocks. There are nine-patch versions, five-patch versions, and some with curved patches. I found nine different patterns with this name. This seven-patch version is shown by Jinny Beyer, who credits it to *Practical Needlework* magazine from around 1910.

Greek Cross

Each page includes a diagram with the make-up of the block to refer to at a glance.

The assembly of four single blocks shows how the pattern works over a larger area of space.

Thumbnail blocks

All the blocks used in this book are displayed here. Use the page references to take you to the relevant instructions for each block.

One-Patch 1

1, p.48

2, p.50

3, p.52

4, p.54

5, p.56

6, p.58

7, p.60

Four-Patch

8, p.62

9, p.64

10, p.66

11, p.68

12, p.70

13, p.72

14, p.74

15, p.76

16, p.78

17, p.80

18, p.82

19, p.84

20, p.86

21, p.88

22, p.90

23, p.92

24, p.94

Five-Patch 3

25, p.96

26, p.98

27, p.100

28, p.102

29, p.104

30, p.106

31, p.108

32, p.110

33, p.112

34, p.114

35, p.116

Seven-Patch 4

36, p.118

37, p.120

38, p.122

39, p.124

40, p.126

41, p.128

42, p.130

Nine-Patch 5

43, p.132

44, p.134

45, p.136

46, p.138

47, p.140

48, p.142

49, p.144

50, p.146

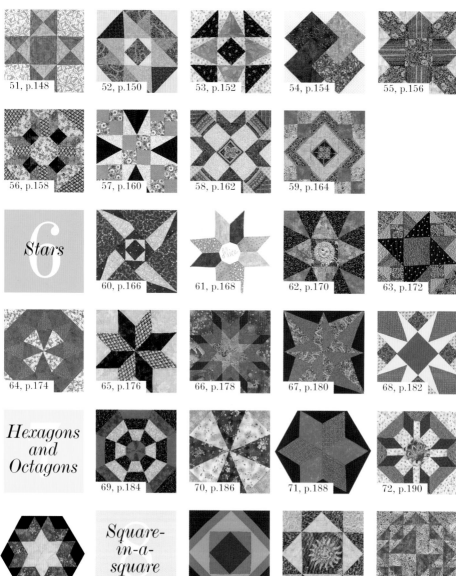

51, p.148

52, p.150

53, p.152

54, p.154

55, p.156

56, p.158

57, p.160

58, p.162

59, p.164

Stars

60, p.166

61, p.168

62, p.170

63, p.172

64, p.174

65, p.176

66, p.178

67, p.180

68, p.182

Hexagons and Octagons

69, p.184

70, p.186

71, p.188

72, p.190

73, p.192

Square-in-a-square

74, p.194

75, p.196

76, p.198

77, p.200

78, p.202

79, p.204

Curved 9

80, p.206

81, p.208

82, p.210

83, p.212

84, p.214

85, p.216

86, p.218

Fans 10

87, p.220

88, p.222

89, p.224

90, p.226

91, p.228

Log Cabin 11

92, p.230

93, p.232

94, p.234

Appliqué 12

95, p.236

96, p.238

97, p.240

98, p.242

99, p.244

100, p.246

Brick Wall

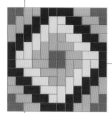

Also known as Brickwork and Old Garden Wall, the earliest published example of this pattern seems to have been in 1854. Although it couldn't be simpler to draft and piece, you can make some interesting designs with it. If you draft it on a large scale, it's ideal for a quick quilt. Four blocks repeated and rotated as shown, make a traditional pattern known as Trip Around the World. You can make many more patterns by changing the colour placements. Notice that you'll need to add squares to the ends of alternate rows to make them even.

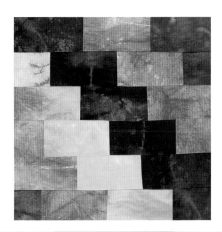

Grandmother's Flower Garden

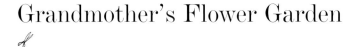

Say 'patchwork' and for many people the hexagon is what comes to mind. It was the 'patch of choice' for the renowned English patchworker, Averil Colby, who brought great artistry to it by her use of colour and patterns. Use a window template or a transparent plastic one, and then select flowers and other designs to build up the pattern.

Joining hexagons together inevitably results in a six-sided shape. So to make a block, cut out a square of background fabric, then carefully position the patchwork in the centre, and appliqué all around it with small, invisible stitches.

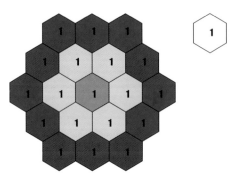

Chevron

This design has been known for hundreds of years and can be seen in heraldic designs, antique tiled floors and ecclesiastical robes. As a patchwork pattern, it has been published under several different names such as Building Blocks, Wave and Rail Fence. The first published sighting of it dates from as early as 1775, according to Ruth Finley, in her book *Old Patchwork Quilts and the Women Who Made Them* (1929). Use it in one of the settings shown, or make a single block for use in a Sampler quilt.

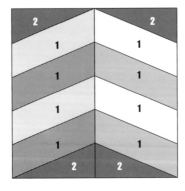

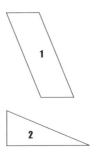

Rail Fence

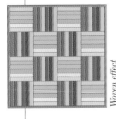

Woven effect

Blocks arranged as steps

Many blocks share the name Rail Fence, but this is
my favourite version for a quick scrap quilt with lots
of possible variations. Use as many or as few strips
and colours as you happen to have around! By
rotating the blocks you can make weaving effects, or
manipulate colours to make steps.

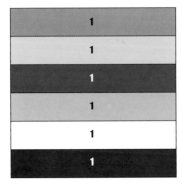

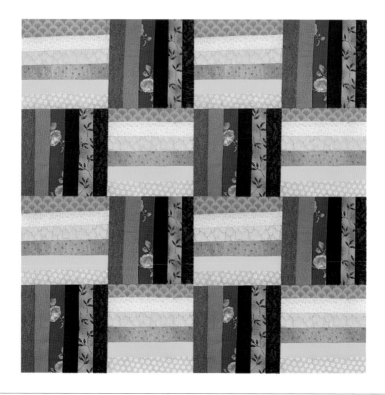

Streak o' Lightning

Repeated triangles create the effect of lightning flashes. This is an old idea for a block, published many times and under many names: Dog's Tooth, Zigzag and Lightning Strips are just a few. Traditionally, it's pieced as a scrap quilt using dark and light triangles. But even such a simple block can produce some interesting designs. You can also vary it by making the triangles from strips.

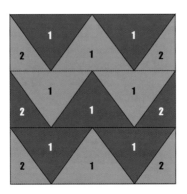

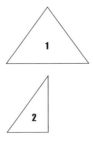

Church Window

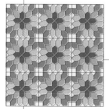

Averil Colby, the first documenter of the English patchwork tradition, refers to any elongated hexagon shape as 'Church Window'. Lucy Boston, the well-known children's author, patchworker and gardener, used a version of it to create the blocks for her famous 'Patchwork of the Crosses', which can still be seen at the Norman manor house near the city of Cambridge, where she lived until her death in 1991. From this one template you can create innumerable patterns. The block is finished by adding a square to each corner and right-angled triangles around the edges.

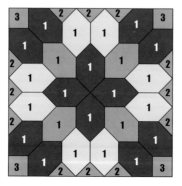

Tumbling Blocks

Also known as Baby Blocks, here's another very familiar patchwork pattern, this time an 'eye fooler' giving a convincing three-dimensional effect when light, dark and medium fabrics are chosen for the diamonds that make up the design. An ideal scrap quilt block, you'll always get the right effect if you stick to the colour rules. Everything depends on the contrast between the three shades.

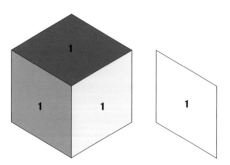

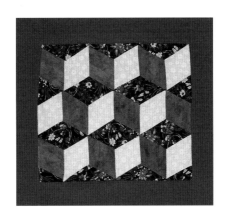

Nelson's *Victory*

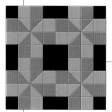

Ruth Finley illustrated this pattern in *Old Patchwork Quilts and the Women Who Made Them* (1929), so it had probably been around a long time before that. Nelson's *Victory* was the ship he commanded at the Battle of Trafalgar in 1805 so who knows, this block may have been around since then, created to celebrate a famous event?

Needing only two templates, this is a simple block to draft and to piece if you follow the illustration for correct colour-placement.

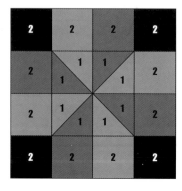

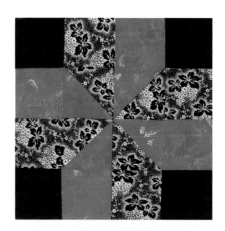

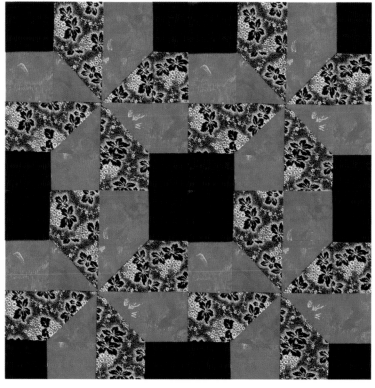

Bow Tie

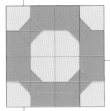

Blocks don't get much easier than this design, which needs only two templates. The Ladies' Art Company published it in 1898 as Necktie and it appeared under the same name in 1929 in the *Kentucky Star*. However, they published it again in 1956 as Bow Tie and that is the name by which it's most commonly known today. Despite its very simple construction, it lends itself to interesting effects if you manipulate the colours.

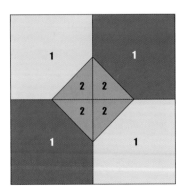
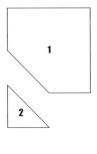

Barbara Fritchie Star

An easy block with a fascinating story behind it, illustrating again that quiltmakers drew their block names and inspiration from many sources, including historical events. At the age of 95, Barbara Fritchie became one of the most famous heroines in American history. During the American Civil War, she staunchly defended her Unionist convictions by refusing to lower the Unionist flag when her hometown was invaded by the Confederates. No threats could persuade her to give in and, so the story is told, she was finally permitted to go on waving it.

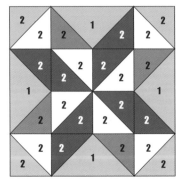
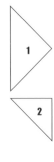

Balkan Puzzle

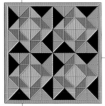

Also known as Windblown Star, this is one of the many block patterns attributed to Nancy Cabot. In fact, 'Nancy Cabot' was a syndicated column written by Loretta Leitner Rising for the *Chicago Tribune* during the 1930s. As for the Balkan part of the name, I can find no explanation for this, although it may be a reference to problems or events that were taking place in the Balkans at the time. Notice that the block is constructed entirely from half-square triangles, so it couldn't be easier to draft and sew.

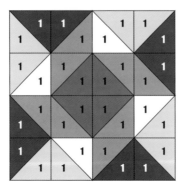

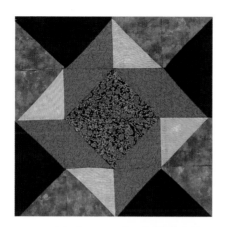

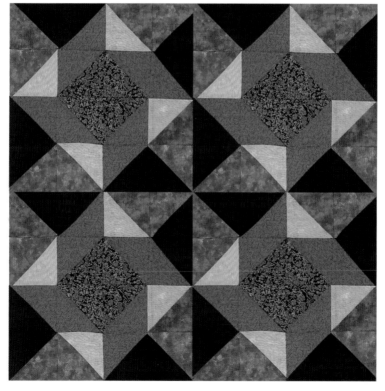

Night and Day

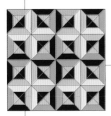

An interesting block from about 1934. It has the alternative name of White Cross but I like the idea of the contrasting dark and light of the title Night and Day which you can reflect in your choice of colours.

As only two templates are needed, the success of the pattern depends on the colour-placement. It's pieced in four sections, which are then joined. I've graded it C because the corner patches need to be 'set in', which needs care.

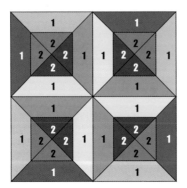
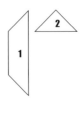

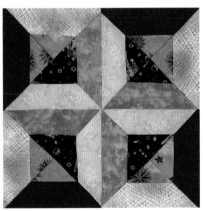

Clay's Choice

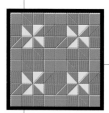

This block is named for the US statesman, Henry Clay (1777–1852). He was known as 'The Great Pacificator' as a result of his genius in the art of compromise. The great national significance of his life is reflected in the proliferation of blocks named for him: Clay's Favourite, Harry's Star and Henry of the West are but a few. The pattern also appears under the names Stardust and Shooting Star. It needs only two templates, a square and a triangle, and is very easy to piece.

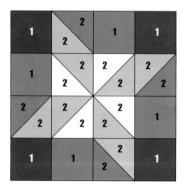

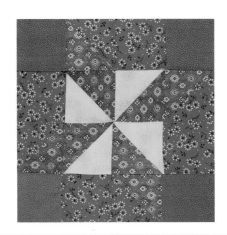

Indian Arrowhead

Many traditional quilt block names reflect the lives of the women who invented them. Understandably, there are lots of blocks with 'Indian' in their names: Indian Hatchet, Indian Summer, Indian Trail and Indian Wedding Ring are just some of them. This one was published in the early 1900s but may have a much older provenance. Although it looks complex, only three templates are needed. Note the colour-placement needed to achieve the right effect.

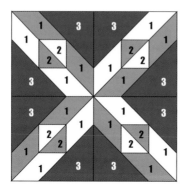

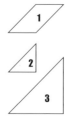

Attic Windows

This block appeared in a needlework magazine in 1857, when it was called Shadow Box. Although only two patches are needed, the design has endless possibilities. The 3-D illusion is easily achieved by making the two frame patches in light and dark colours respectively.

Four units are shown as one block, which works well in a Sampler quilt. It's very quick to make but take care with the mitred corners. Remember the secret is to stitch exactly up to, but NOT into the seam allowance.

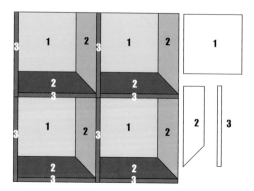

Kentucky Chain

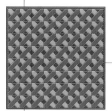

Jinny Beyer records that *Practical Needlework* first published this pattern in about 1910. The US state of Kentucky has given its name to several blocks, many of which are just variations on other blocks, but this one seems to be unique.

Although it may look complex, it is very simple to piece. The interlacing, or lattice, effect adds interest and you'll achieve the best impression of this by alternating dark and light fabrics for the over and under patches. It makes a great scrap quilt if you just follow the 'light/dark' fabric rule.

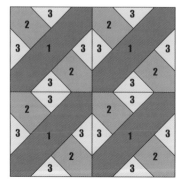
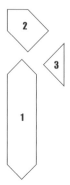

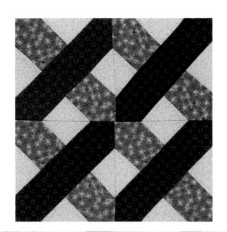

Trailing Star

The Ladies' Art Company, probably the first mail-order suppliers of quilt patterns, published this block under the name Old Poinsettia in 1895. Nancy Cabot also called it Spinning Star, but by 1982 it appears as Trailing Star. I always use that name for it because it's such a good description of the block.

Draft the block on a 4 x 4 grid. Make four identical units, making sure that you cut out all the patches with the templates the same way up. DON'T cut patches from two layers of fabric placed wrong-sides together or your 'star' won't work.

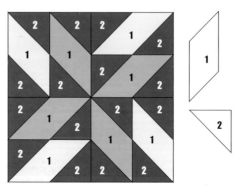

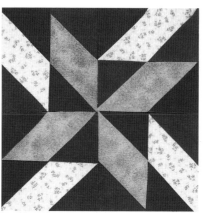

Double Pinwheel

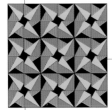

Many patchwork blocks are called Pinwheels and they vary in construction from the simplest to the most complex. This is a variation that I made years ago, but haven't been able to track down in any of the standard works. Although it needs five templates, they go together very easily so it's not difficult to piece. Notice that the four sections are identical, so piece each one and then join them to form the block.

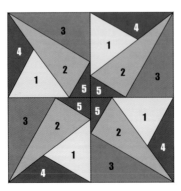

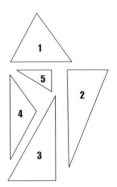

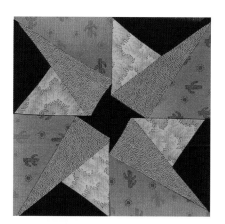

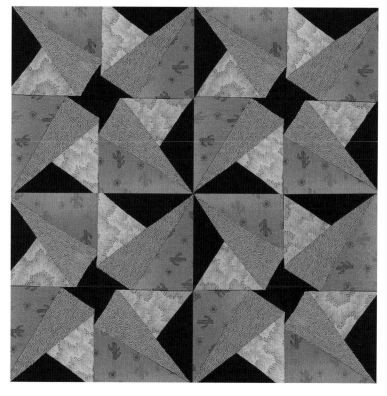

Four-Patch Weave

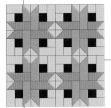

I've looked for this block in all the usual sources and references but have only managed to locate it in one place: the blocks library of the very first computer quilt program I ever owned. It was listed simply as Four-Patch Block, so I've given it a descriptive name to suit the design. You'll see that the full block is constructed from four identical units, needing five templates. Despite its lack of provenance, this is a good block on which to practise your design skills. For example, try changing the colours in the patches at each corner.

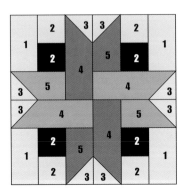

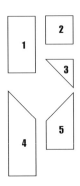

Storm at Sea

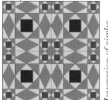

Impression of circles

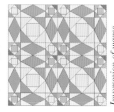

Colour variation

Impression of waves

A very popular traditional block with wonderful design possibilities. In repeated blocks the long triangles on each side appear to join to give an illusion of circles. You can ring many changes on the pattern by playing with the colours. I've graded this block C because of the number of templates and patches involved, although the piecing isn't as complicated as it looks.

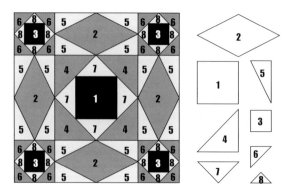

Dogtooth Violet

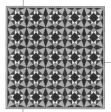

If you've seen a real dogtooth violet, you'll see that this pattern is well named. The triangles in each corner remind me of the shapes of the petals. This is another block attributed to Nancy Cabot, dating from the 1930s.

Draft the block on an 8 x 8 grid. Try to cut the outer-triangle patches so that the longest edge is on the straight grain of the fabric, otherwise they'll stretch and distort the final measurement of the block. First piece the whole centre star as shown. Then piece the four corner blocks and join them to the centre.

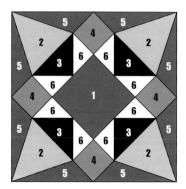

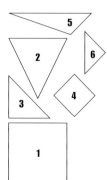

Northumberland Star

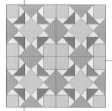

All the reference books agree on the name of this block and it doesn't seem to be known by any alternative names. Perhaps Northumberland Star was so named by the inhabitants of Northumberland, Pennsylvania, USA. It's also possible that it may be a very early block christened by the settlers from Northumberland in northern England, many of whom emigrated to that part of the USA. Its nearest relation appears to be a block published by Ruby McKim in 1929 as Wild Goose, which it closely resembles. It's easily drafted on a 16 x 16 grid and needs five templates and four fabrics.

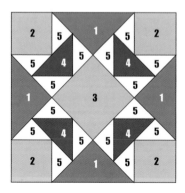
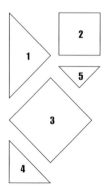

Key West Beauty

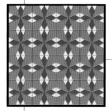

Another delightful block published in 1928 by the Ladies' Art Company, Key West Beauty is also known as Key West Star and Dakota Star. Piece it in four identical sections as shown, then join them. Accurate piecing is needed to ensure that the points meet neatly in the centre.

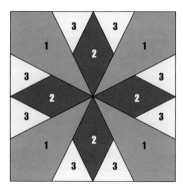

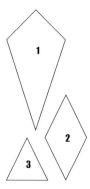

Diamond Star

Diamond Star was the name given to this block by a farming
magazine in 1930, but it has since appeared as Amethyst,
Windmill Star and Diamond Wedding Quilt Block. It's a typical
'eye fooler' because although there are no curved seams to sew, an
optical illusion of curves is created. Note the light/dark colour
placement, which will enhance the effect of interlocking circles.
Make the block up in four units, then join them two at a time.
I've graded this block C because care is needed in joining the four
units together so that you get nice sharp points in the centre.

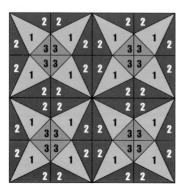

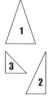

Grandmother's Choice

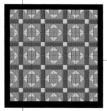

Published in 1899 by the Ladies' Art Company, this easy block has many other names: Duck and Duckling, Corn and Beans, Handy Andy and Hen and Chickens. Use bold-patterned fabric to add interest to what is a very straightforward block – perfect for beginners.

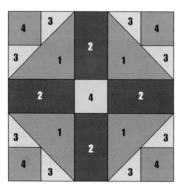

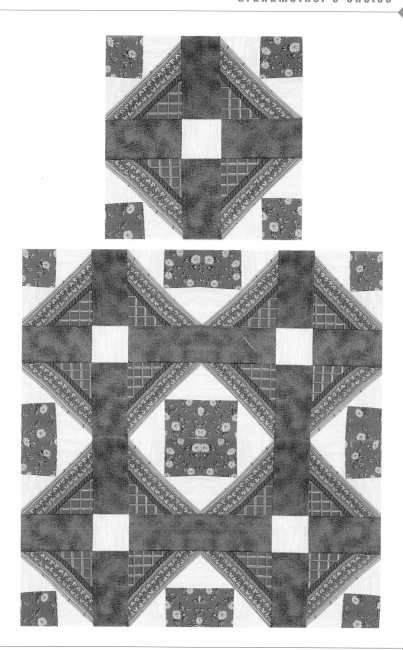

Minnesota

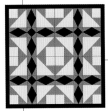

This block was originally published by the periodical *Hearth and Home*, which appeared from 1885 until the 1930s, although I cannot find any exact date for its publication. The piecing of the central 'cross', seen in most five-patch blocks, adds interesting complexity to an otherwise plain block.

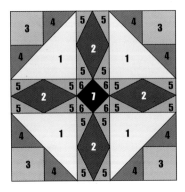 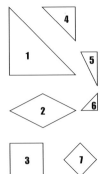

Cross and Crown

This is a traditional block known also as Bouquet and Goose Tracks. Ruth Finley dates it from 1935, but there are versions of it from much earlier dates. Try using a striped fabric for the large rhombus-shaped patches to emphasise the effect of a square overlaid by a cross.

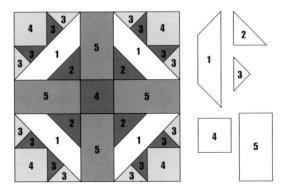

Jack in the Box

Straight set

Emphasis of central star

According to Jinny Beyer, this block dates from 1931. Notice the 'star' effect in the centre when four blocks are repeated. You could emphasise this by varying the colours in the patches where the four blocks meet.

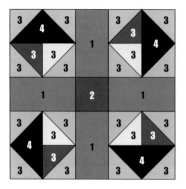

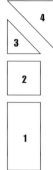

Celia's Pinwheel Square

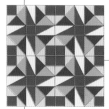

My block is a variation on the traditional Follow the Leader, also published by the Ladies' Art Company as Pinwheel Square in 1898. Again, the design is created by sub-dividing the central square, adding complexity and movement. Try drafting the block yourself and making some more adaptations of your own.

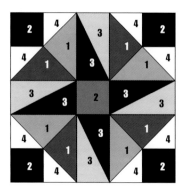

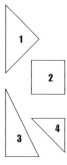

Lady of the Lake

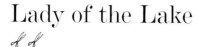

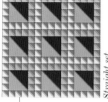

Straight set

Blocks rotated 90°

Lady of the Lake was published in 1898 by the Ladies' Art Company and has been a firm favourite ever since. It's a deceptively simple block, needing only two templates, yet has lots of design potential. Look carefully at the light/dark fabric placing to get the most striking effects.

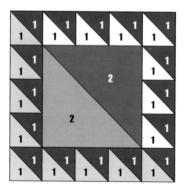

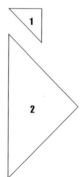

Pine Tree

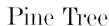

Block names taken from the natural world abound, and pine trees are especially popular, so there are many blocks of this name. This particular version was a Grandmother Clark design, so probably dates from the end of the nineteenth century. You can use up lots of scraps of green patterned fabrics if you want to keep the 'evergreen' theme. Another popular way of using the block in a quilt is to alternate it with plain muslin blocks which can be quilted with a variety of patterns.

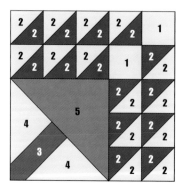

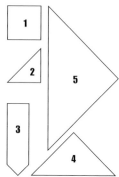

Providence Block

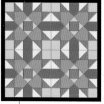

Straight set

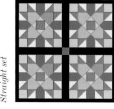

Set with sashings

Another turn of the century block, it is probably named Providence after the town of that name in Kentucky, USA. Of course, it might also refer to the thrifty motives that were once important aspects of the activities of patchwork and quilting!

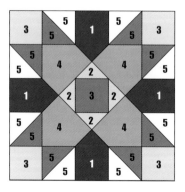

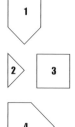

Georgia

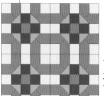

Straight set

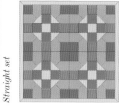

Colour variation

I could find only one source of this delightful pattern, *Hearth and Home*, suggesting that it probably dates from the end of the nineteenth century. We can only speculate on the derivation of the name: like many blocks, it could have been named after the place where it was created, or else, like many another block, from the name of its maker. Notice the 'set in' seams for the corner blocks.

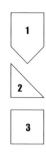

Bull's Eye

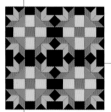

Bull's Eye has many names, such as Doe and Darts, David and Goliath, Flying Darts and Four Darts, so I think we can say that it's been around for a very long time. You need to draft it on a 25 x 25 grid. In each corner, the square and triangles on the outer edge have 'set in' seams – look at the basic instructions given for how to do this. If you piece the corner sections first, the rest is easy.

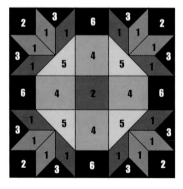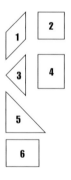

Turkey Tracks

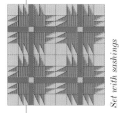

Set with sashings

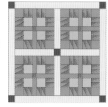

Set with posts

Understandably, turkeys feature quite frequently in the names of American patchwork blocks; there are Turkey Giblets, Turkey in the Straw and this one. It's easily drafted on a 10 x 10 grid, but the small triangle patches need careful piecing.

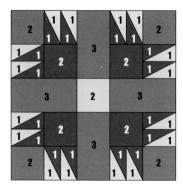

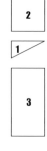

Walls of Jericho

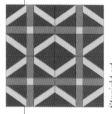

Straight set

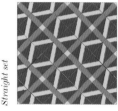

On point set

Another block with a name derived from biblical sources. A similar version was shown by Nancy Cabot in 1935 but I found this one in Maggie Malone's *1001 Patchwork Designs* (1982). It's a deceptively simple design that is very easy to piece, but repeated blocks make interesting subsidiary patterns, especially when set 'on point'. It also makes a good scrap quilt if you use a variety of fabrics for the diagonal stripes but unify them by using a single colour for the background and for the bars.

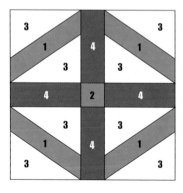

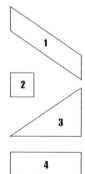

Country Roads

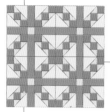

Martha Marshall includes this block under the name of Buffalo Ridge in her book *Quilts of Appalachia: the Mountain Woman and Her Quilts* (1972). This suggests that the pattern may date from the early to mid-nineteenth century, when there was a huge increase in westward migration into and over the Appalachian Mountains, USA. The block also appeared as Country Roads in 1979, in *Quilt World* magazine. Perhaps the name is taken from the well-known Country and Western song of that name. Piece the four corners first, then join them with the centre bars.

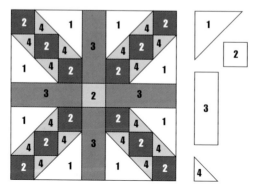

Greek Cross

Greek Cross is a popular, generic name for blocks.
There are nine-patch versions, five-patch versions
and some with curved patches; I found nine
different patterns with this name. This seven-patch
version is shown by Jinny Beyer, who credits it to
Practical Needlework magazine from around 1910.

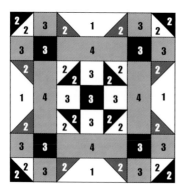
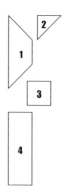

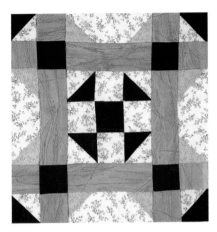

Lincoln's Platform

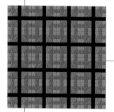

Here's another block whose name has political connotations. A version of it was published by The Ladies' Art Company in 1898, thirty-three years after Abraham Lincoln's assassination, so it seems likely that it had been around as a traditional block for many years before it got into print.

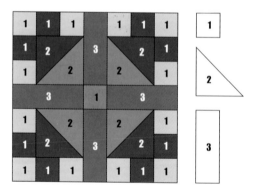

Rosebud

This is a Nancy Page design, dating from between 1920 and 1930. Repeated blocks give the effect of a pieced star block with sashings, with the added bonus that you don't have to add sashings to all the finished blocks!

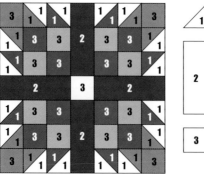

North Carolina Lily

Petals pointing inward

Stems pointing inward

There are many different North Carolina Lily blocks, but this particular version is one I found in a remarkable quilt now in the museum in Guernsey, one of the Channel Islands. The original quilt is pieced entirely in reds and greens and is quilted in a style of stuffed quilting, or trapunto, which characterised many quilts in that region and time. This is a tricky block to piece and it's easiest sewn by hand, although you can machine stitch it with care. Being a-symmetrical, you can get two completely different quilts by rotating the blocks.

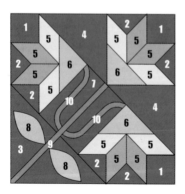

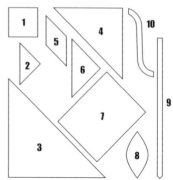

Dove in the Window

Doves were popular in block names and appear quite
often. For example, Dove at the Window, Dove at the
Crossroads and Dove of Peace are variations. There are
two quite different blocks called Dove in the Window, but
this is the version which was published by the Ladies'
Art Company in 1898, and which also appears in *The
Romance of the Patchwork Quilt* (1935).

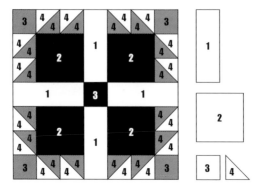

Churn Dash

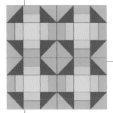

This is surely one of the oldest and most popular of the traditional blocks, and it is also delightfully easy to make. Barbara Brackman lists as many as 18 different names for it, although Churn Dash seems to be the most popular. Alternatives include Broken Plate, Double Monkey Wrench, Fisherman's Reel, Hole in the Barn Door and Indian Hammer.

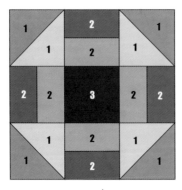

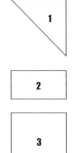

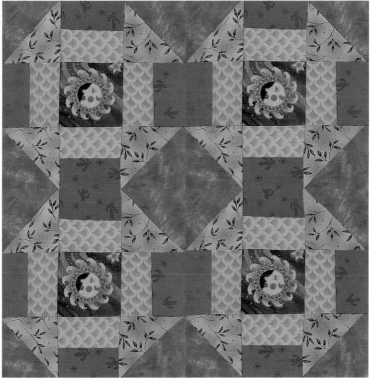

Cat's Cradle

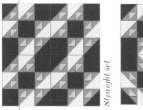

Straight set

Blocks rotated 90°

This block has so many names it's impossible to list them all: Double Pyramids, Dove at the Window, Flying Birds, Hour Glass and Wandering Lover are just some of them. Perhaps that final name was given by some young woman abandoned by her fickle sweetheart! The earliest published date I can find for it is 1895, but I suspect that it's much older than that. This is an easy block, so it's perfect for beginners. Notice the interesting effects obtained by rotating the block.

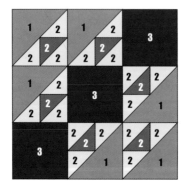

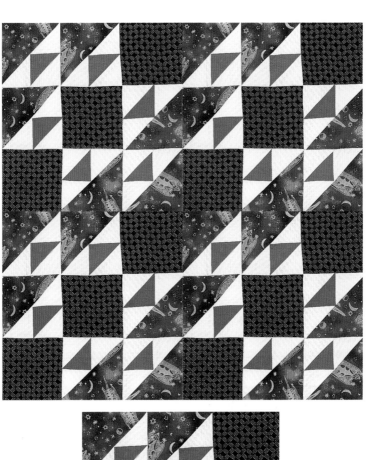

Ribbon Quilt Block

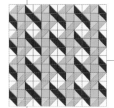

This block is attributed to Nancy Page. Nancy Page
was in fact a syndicated mail-order column which
appeared between the 1920s and 1940s. It's another
very simple nine-patch with a built-in 'eye fooler'
effect if you place dark and light fabrics as shown.
It also makes a lovely scrap quilt.

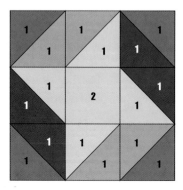

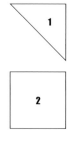

Nine-Patch Frame

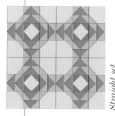

Straight set

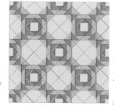

On point set

Here's an adaptation that I have made of a block
in Maggie Malone's book, *1001 Patchwork Designs*.
So far I haven't found the original in any other
source books, so I'm unable to give its history. But
it looks particularly effective in a quilt in an 'on
point' setting.

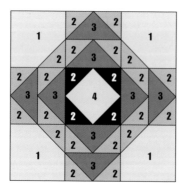

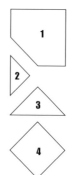

Celia's Nifty Nine-Patch

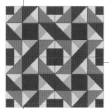

Here's a block I made up, and since I can't find it in any of the usual sources, I've 'adopted' it as my own. If you follow the dark/light fabric placement shown repeated blocks will always have the interesting 'cross-over' effect. I called it 'Nifty' because I discovered that with some simple adaptations I could turn it into at least three different nine-patch blocks, each of which made an interesting quilt. It's drafted on an 18 x 18 grid.

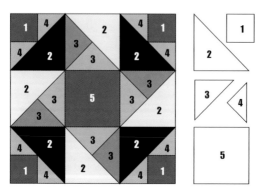

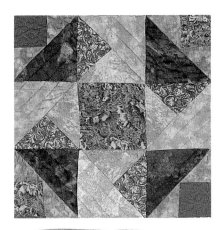

Shaded Nine-Patch

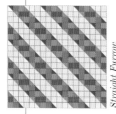

Straight Furrow

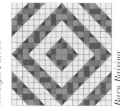

Barn Raising

One simple nine-patch block makes many quilts! This is the ultimate scrap quilt block on which many variations are possible. By rotating the blocks to manipulate the dark/light sides you can create several pleasing effects. The settings shown are traditional arrangements, which are the basis of the famous Log Cabin quilts (see page 230) and the names are expressive of the graphic effects achieved. Straight Furrow resembles the paths of a ploughed field, while Barn Raising is supposed to resemble the laid-out sections of a barn when it's assembled on the ground before it's erected.

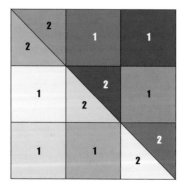

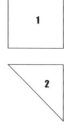

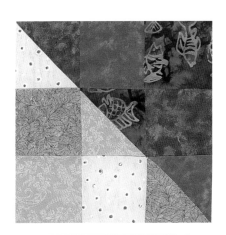

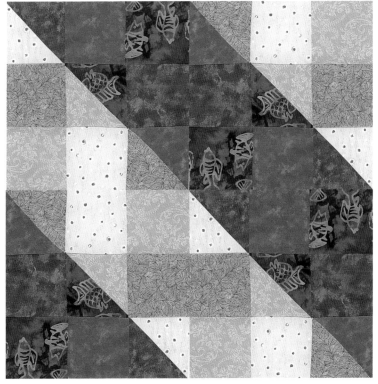

The Road to Paradise

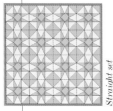

Straight set

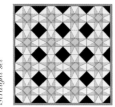

Black corner patches

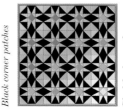

Black backgrounds

Farm Journal, a periodical which began publication in 1877 and which I believe is still publishing, called this block Doris's Delight but I found it under the name Road to Paradise in Beth Gutcheon's book, *The Perfect Patchwork Primer.* It's a block which demonstrates beautifully the design strengths of the simple nine-patch block. Repeated blocks give an illusion of interlocking curves. You can achieve an entirely different effect by swapping the pale background patches for black, and yet another simply by making all the corner blocks black. Only five templates are needed and the piecing is straightforward.

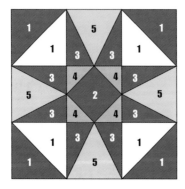

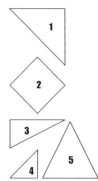

Jacob's Ladder

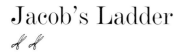

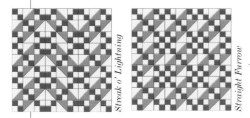

Streak o' Lightning

Straight Furrow

One of the oldest traditional blocks, Jacob's Ladder is also one of the many blocks with biblical names. But it has many other names, such as Underground Railway, referring to the system of secret routes by which slaves could escape from captivity in the South of the USA. Needing only two templates, this is another good block for a beginner. Note the variation in pattern when alternate blocks are rotated.

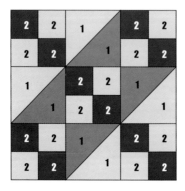

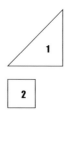

Ohio Star

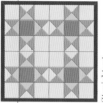

Straight set

On point set

On point with sashings

No book of blocks would be complete without Ohio Star, a
top favourite nine-patch with generations of patchworkers
and quilters. It makes a wonderful scrap quilt, for example,
making each block from scraps of one colour. You can set
this block with sashings, with alternate plain blocks or
simply place the blocks together – whatever setting you use,
you'll always have a classic patchwork quilt.

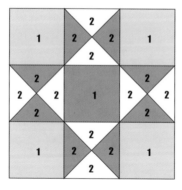

Air Castle

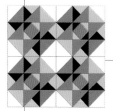

Air Castle is a Ladies' Art Company block, which was first published in 1898. It is also the romantically named Towers of Camelot, although I have not discovered any explanation for either name.

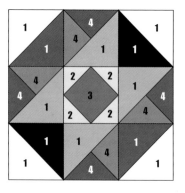
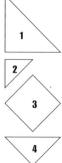

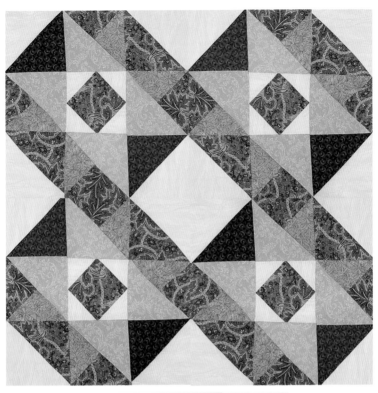

Little Rock Block

This is my adaptation of Little Rock Block, which is the name under which the Ladies' Art Company published it in 1928. Nancy Cabot subsequently published it as Butterfly Block and Star of the Sea during the 1930s. It is named after the town of Little Rock, Arkansas, USA, and in fact sometimes appears as Arkansas Star.

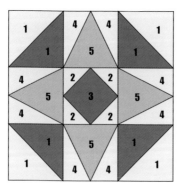

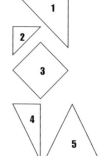

Card Trick

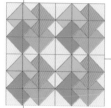

This is my variation on Card Trick, a relatively modern block first published in Beth Gutcheon's *The Perfect Patchwork Primer* in 1976. (It's actually copyrighted to Jeff Gutcheon.) Interestingly for such a recent addition to the blocks repertoire, it's become a standard classic, invariably seen in Sampler quilts. I've amended it a little to emphasise the way in which the colours and shapes interlock. You'll see that it only needs two templates, but care is needed in placement of the colours to achieve the right effect.

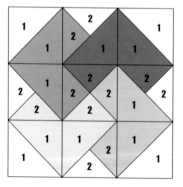

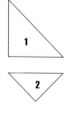

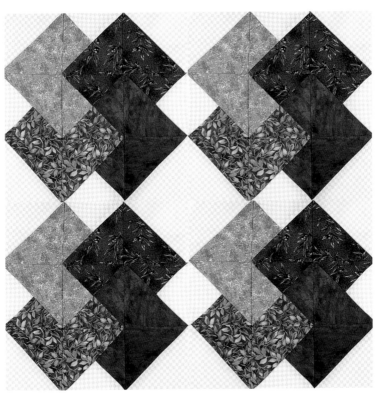

Prairie Flower

Prairie Flower is attributed to Nancy Cabot, so it almost certainly dates from the 1930s. Several blocks feature prairie in their name, perhaps christened by the pioneering women who took their needlecraft skills with them on the long, hazardous treks to the West of the USA in the mid- to late nineteenth century, particularly when Oregon Fever in the mid-1840s set thousands of emigrants on the Oregon Trail.

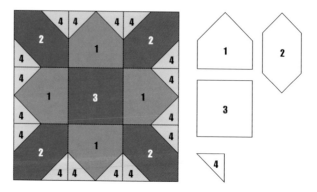

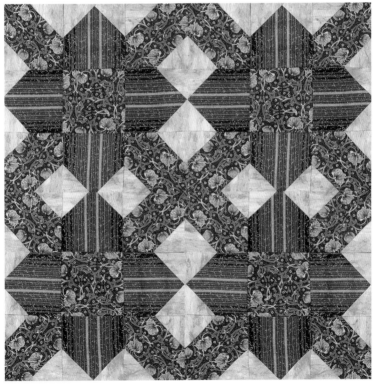

Prosperity Block

All the usual reference sources are agreed that this is another Nancy Cabot block, dating from the early 1930s. It needs a 36 x 36 grid, but don't be daunted by that, because once you've got the grid it's really very easy to draft. Note that the centre units on each side have 'set in' seams (see page 28).

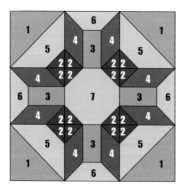

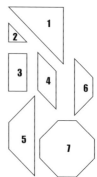

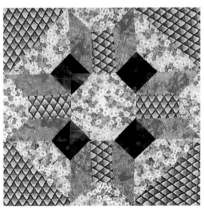

Fifty-Four–Forty or Fight

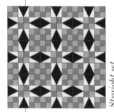

Straight set

On point set

This is one of the many blocks named to commemorate political events. 'Fifty-Four–Forty or Fight' was a slogan used during the dispute between the USA and Britain over the boundaries of Oregon. The USA maintained its right of sovereignty of the whole region up to latitude 50° 40' N. In 1844, the slogan was successfully used by Democrat James K. Polk in his campaign to be president.

The block has been published under other names, for example, *The Rural New Yorker* published it as The Railroad Quilt in 1934, but Fifty-Four–Forty or Fight is its most popular and widely known name.

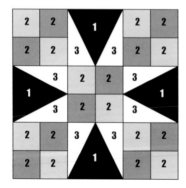

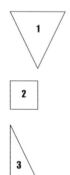

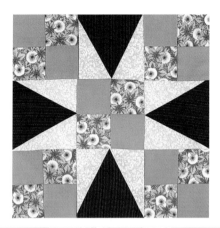

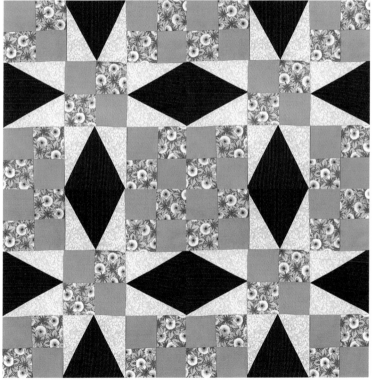

Swing in the Centre

Quilt makers have traditionally drawn inspiration from anything and everything around them. Here's a block which neatly illustrates this point, as its name is a reference to a square-dancing formation, where the caller instructs a set of dancers to hold hands and 'swing in the centre'. The pattern appeared as Roman Pavement in the *Chicago Tribune* in the 1930s and has several other names, such as Mrs. Roosevelt's Favourite. Piece the block in three sections as shown below, and then join them together.

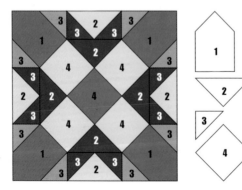

Aunt Sukey's Choice

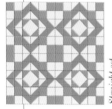
Straight set

On point set

There are several older blocks attributed to 'Aunt Sukey' but this is my version, which is based on one published in 1935 in *The Romance of the Patchwork Quilt*. The block looks interestingly complex, but in fact the construction is very simple. Lots of different effects can be obtained simply by varying the colours.

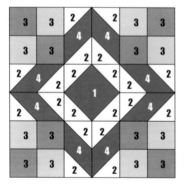

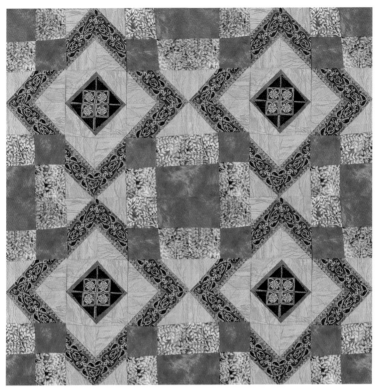

Eccentric Star

An interesting block illustrated in Jonathan Holstein's classic book, *The Pieced Quilt: an American Design Tradition*, in a Pennsylvania quilt dated approximately 1910. Although there are a few traditional blocks with similar features, this appears to be a unique example of folk art ingenuity as it doesn't appear in any of the earlier sources of block patterns. This is one block which you might find easier to piece by hand than by machine. You can easily draft it on a 24 x 24 grid. Don't be daunted by the number of templates needed – the block goes together quite easily if you piece the centre square-in-a-square first.

 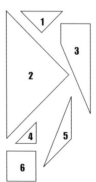

Friendship Star

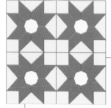

A Friendship Star is usually one with enough space in the centre for names to be written in it. Traditionally, it was a popular way of making a quilt as a parting gift. This particular pattern appeared in the *Kansas City Star* in 1933 and is ideal for the purpose. The 'petals' can be made in scrap fabrics on a single, unifying background fabric but the centre should be of plain muslin.

The centre patch is an octagon, which is best appliquéd into position when the petals have been pieced.

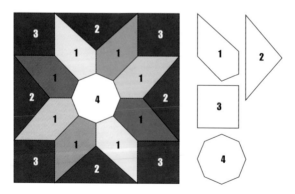

Guiding Star

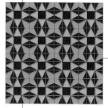

I've adapted this block from one which appeared as
Guiding Star in the *Kansas City Star* in 1933. My version
is much easier to piece but is still, I think, very effective.
Draft it on a 24 x 24 grid. The piecing isn't difficult, but
accuracy is needed to get good points where the corner
squares join those at the sides. Carefully check each patch
with the template and make sure that your ½ cm (¼ inch)
seam allowance is exact (see page 28). This is yet another
of the many blocks which give a pleasing illusion of
interlocked circles when repeated over the quilt surface.

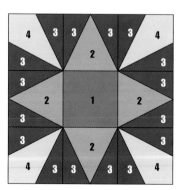

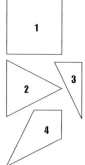

Nifty Star

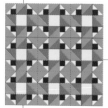

The Nifty Star is really a nine-patch star, developed from Celia's Nifty Nine-Patch (see page 126). I liked the way a little adjustment of the units within the block produced a distinctive star effect. You'll see that each unit was rotated by 180°. Look at the diagrams to see how I did it. You can do this with lots of blocks constructed from clearly defined units to create your own unique blocks. Why not try it yourself?

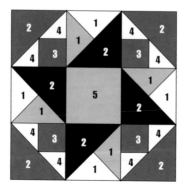
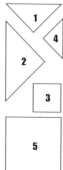

Morning Star

of of of

This could just as easily be described as an octagon block, as it is based on the familiar Kaleidoscope block which is constructed from eight identical triangles. In this case, however, the triangles have been subdivided to create a more complex block. *The Kansas City Star* first published it in 1931 as Evening Star, but when they re-published it in 1959 it was called Spider Web Gone Awry and if you look at the Spider Web block in the Hexagons and Octagons section (page 184), you'll see what they meant!

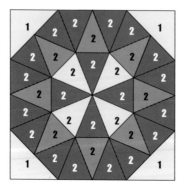

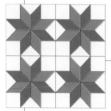

Star of Le Moyne

d d d

The name of this block commemorates two French explorers,
the brothers Pierre and Jean Baptiste Le Moyne. They
explored the Mississippi River and in 1718 founded the city
of New Orleans, where we can guess that this block would
have been named. In the North of America, among non-
French-speaking quilters, Le Moyne has been corrupted into
Lemon Star and there's a long list of other names to choose
from. The construction is simply eight, 60° diamond shapes,
with half-squares and squares set into the corners. You can
either draft it on a 40 x 40 grid, or use a compass and ruler.

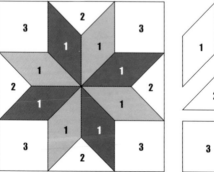

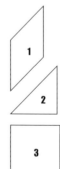

Virginia Star

There are many variations on this eight-pointed pieced star. It appeared in 1935 as Virginia Star in *The Romance of the Patchwork Quilt*, although Jinny Beyer credits it to a magazine called *Quilting* in 1934. This block is much easier to piece than it looks. Piece and join the centre star first, then set in the surrounding squares and triangles. To draft it, use a 40 x 40 grid. However, another, perhaps easier method, is to use a compass and draw a circle with a 15cm (6 inch) radius. Divide it into eight sections, then join the points. You can draft lots of eight-pointed stars like this, so it's a useful technique to learn.

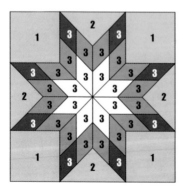 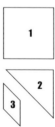

Blazing Star

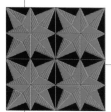

Blazing Star is another block which seems to have been adopted by patchworkers in the 1930s, although it is a design often seen in ancient pavements and tiles. The block appears in *The Romance of the Patchwork Quilt* (1935) under this name and also as Four-Pointed Star. Other names include Mother's Delight and St. Louis Star. It is possible to draft it on a 40 x 40 grid, but it's much better to use the compass and ruler method. Note how the templates are used. Each one must be used twice, once reversed, to make each point of the star.

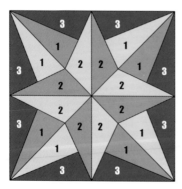
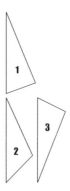

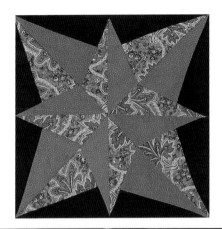

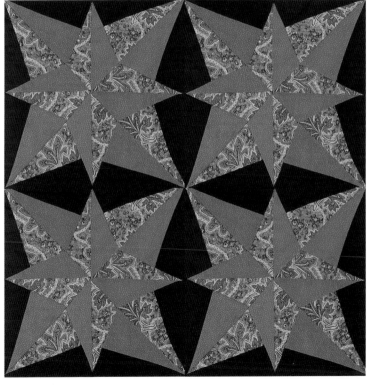

1904 Star

Straight set

On point set

This is a slight adaptation of a star block first published in a *Practical Needlework* booklet around 1910. It's an unusual star which doesn't seem to have been published very often, although it has great design potential. Repeated blocks form circles around four-pointed stars, while an 'on point' setting brings out the four star shapes.

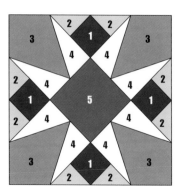

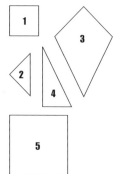

Spider Web

Jinny Beyer credits this block to *Grandmother Clark's Authentic Early American Quilts*, which was one of a series of booklets published by W.M.L.Clark of St. Louis, beginning in the 1930s. It's really a variation on the Kaleidoscope block, created by joining eight, 45° triangles.

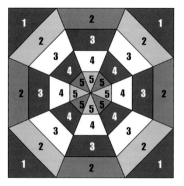 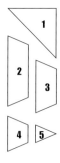

Kaleidoscope

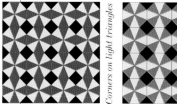
Corners on light triangles

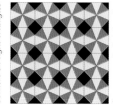
Corners on dark triangles

The Ladies' Art Company published this block as Kaleidoscope in 1898. But it has appeared under a whole list of alternative names, including Octagons, Willow the Wisp and my favourite, Parquetry for a Quilt Block.

This block is easy to construct on a 24 x 24 grid. You'll see that the block is basically an octagon made up of eight, 45° triangles; by adding right-angled triangles to four sides, the octagon becomes a square. You get the best effects by alternating dark and light fabrics for the triangles, which makes this an ideal scrap quilt block.

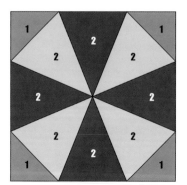

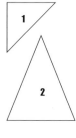

Six-sided Star

Published by *Practical Needlework* around 1910, this is
one of my favourite blocks for a scrap quilt. You can
stitch the blocks by machine but you have to set in the
triangles on each side. The best method to use is
English Patchwork (see page 31 for basic instructions).
This method also makes joining the completed blocks
very simple. If you decide to piece by machine, join the
blocks in rows, taking great care to set in the seams as
you go.

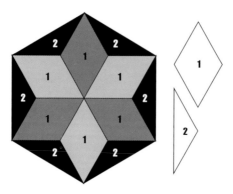

Miss Jackson

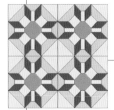

The Ladies' Art Company first published this block as Miss Jackson in 1922. Nancy Page called it Empty Spools and the *Detroit Free Press* called it Wisconsin Star. Miss Jackson certainly isn't the easiest block to piece and you may prefer to sew it by hand. However, it is such a beautiful block that it's well worth the extra trouble. It can easily be drafted on a 24 x 24 grid.

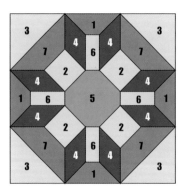

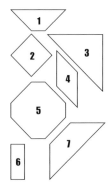

The Columbia

Once again, the Ladies' Art Company seems to have been the first to actually publish this traditional pattern, but it has subsequently appeared quite often, sometimes called Columbian Star. It's another ideal block for a scrap quilt since the effect of the pattern is achieved entirely from the placing of the dark, light and medium fabrics. You'll see that it needs only two templates, a triangle and a 60° diamond. To make the pattern into a rectangle, just add plain triangles then a border. Alternatively, this design is very effective if you appliqué each hexagon onto a square background block.

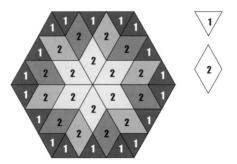

Amish Style

The Amish, or Plain People, came to the United States in the early eighteenth century. They were a sect of the Mennonite church and had been subjected to religious persecution in Europe. The basis of their belief was a strict adherence to the Bible and a commitment to Christian living.

In contrast to their sober way of life, their quilts are made using strong, vibrant colours. Black is also often used for greater contrast. Their designs tend to be large, plain geometrical layouts. This block reflects some of the features of a typical Amish quilt.

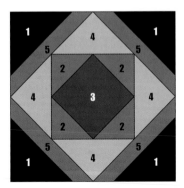

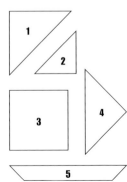

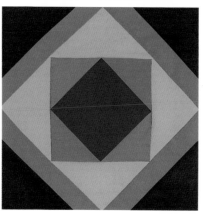

Art Square

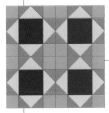

Published as Art Square by the Ladies' Art Company in 1898, this block was later published by the *Farm Journal* as Dottie's Choice and is also known as Village Square. It makes a good block for a beginner or for a quick quilt. For the centre square choose a really striking fabric to give your quilt a strong focus, or showcase a conversation fabric there.

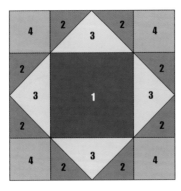

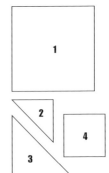

Corn and Beans

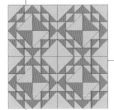

Another traditional block with many names, of which Corn and Beans is just one. The Ladies' Art Company, publishing it in 1898, called it by that name but Carrie Hall, in *The Romance of the Patchwork Quilt* (1935), gives it various other names as well, including Duck and Ducklings, Handy Andy, Hen and Chickens and Crazy Ann. She writes that this particular block was the pattern used for a quilt in the first Farm Demonstration Home, in Missouri, USA, attesting to its long-standing popularity.

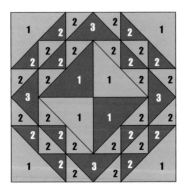

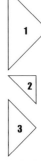

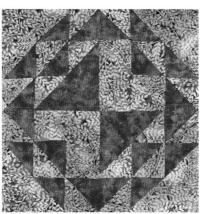

Double Squares

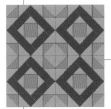

A traditional block first published in 1898 by The Ladies' Art Company and subsequently appearing under several other names. In 1918, *Needlecraft Magazine* called it Broken Dishes and in 1944 the *Kansas City Star* published it as Jack in the Pulpit. Piece the centre square first, then piece each of the four corners as separate units and attach them to the square.

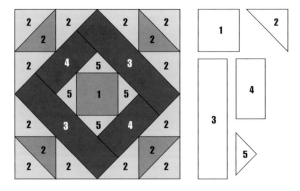

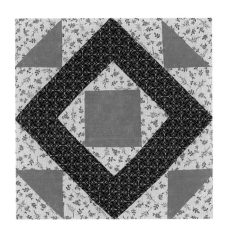

Virginia Reel

Straight set

Blocks rotated 90°

A variation on a traditional block known as Snail Trail, this particular version was published by *Mountain Mist,* both as Virginia Reel and as Pig's Tail. Virginia Reel is a fascinating block from which you can make two very different quilts just by rotating alternate blocks by 90°. It also makes a good scrap quilt if you choose fabrics to emphasise the dark/light contrast. Although it needs six templates, there's nothing very difficult in the construction – just start from the centre square and work out.

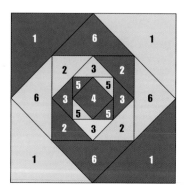

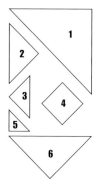

Broken Band

Barbara Brackenbridge mentions only one place
where this block has been published and that was in
Farm News in 1920. This was a farming magazine
that first appeared in the early twentieth century,
and I haven't been able to track it down in any other
sources. I think it's unjustly neglected because
although it's simple to piece, the repeated blocks
produce a particularly striking graphic effect and
make an interesting quilt.

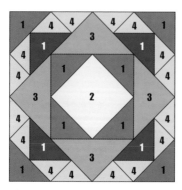

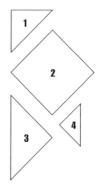

Bleeding Hearts

An interesting block dating from the 1920s or '30s. The Ladies' Art Company published a slight variation of it in 1928, which Hall and Kretsinger included in their book *The Romance of the Patchwork Quilt* (1935). You can either piece it by hand, or appliqué the shapes to a background square. Repeated blocks make it one of the best eye fooler quilts I know.

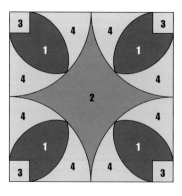

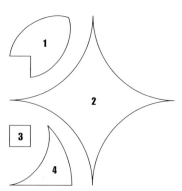

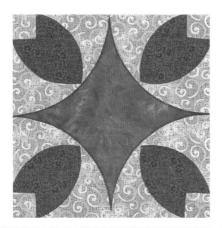

Melon Patch

As Ruth Finley says, this block comes 'straight out of the old-time flower and vegetable gardens'. It is one of several blocks with curves which get their effect from a counter-change of colours in the background and the main design shapes, and there are many variations on it. The Ladies' Art Company published it in 1898 as Orange Peel and it's also known as Lafayette Orange Peel. *Woman's World* magazine published it in 1931 as Flower Petals. The easiest way to draft this block is with a compass.

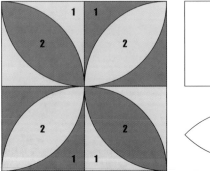

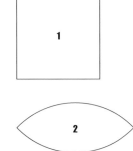

Tobacco Leaf

This is a variation of a Nancy Cabot block, which Maggie Malone illustrates. However, I haven't been able to find it in any of the other sources so, as with many traditional blocks, the name of the original inventor remains a mystery! The best way to create this block is by a combination of piecing and appliqué. First piece the square-in-a-square then appliqué the large, curved 'petals' over it. It makes an excellent scrap quilt if you keep the same colours for the background squares but make the petals of random fabrics.

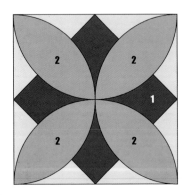

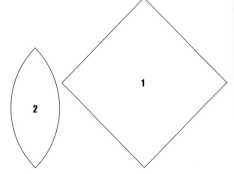

Drunkard's Path

This is a wonderfully simple idea for a block yet it
provides some varied and interesting quilt designs. The
basic unit, as shown in the diagrams, can be repeated
and rotated in several ways to make distinctively
different patterns. Arranged as in the block illustrated,
it has many names, including Old Maid's Puzzle and
Solomon's Puzzle. To make the block shown you need
to make eight of each colour-way of the basic unit, so
sixteen units altogether. By rotating and re-arranging
the units you can create several different blocks.

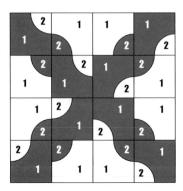

Winding Ways

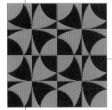

Another block with many aliases. The Ladies' Art Company was apparently the first to publish it under the name of Winding Ways in 1928. Since then it has appeared variously as Four Leaf Clover, Nashville and Robbing Peter to Pay Paul. Ruth Finley calls it Wheel of Mystery and says that if you make sure to emphasise the contrasting colours, then your quilt will be 'a thing of beauty and a joy for ever'! Winding Ways is the name by which it is most familiar today.

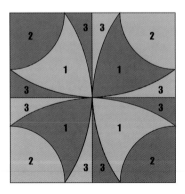

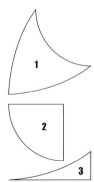

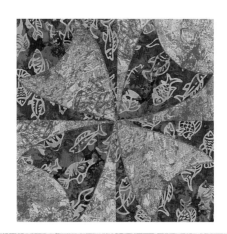

Nocturne

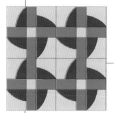

A delightful example of original design, this modern
block was first published by Nancy Cabot in 1934. It
has obviously gained some popularity since Maggie
Malone illustrates it in *1001 Patchwork Patterns*
(1982). Because the curved patches are quite shallow,
this is a lot easier to piece than it may look.

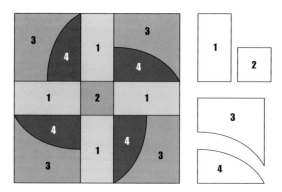

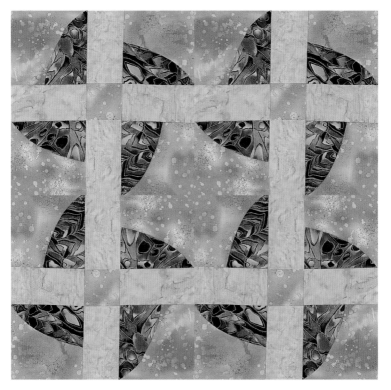

Peter and Paul

Here's a block with a long pedigree. In her classic book
Patchwork (1958), Averil Colby tells us that this block was
known in Somerset as Peter and Paul. Hall and Kretsinger
called it Robbing Peter to Pay Paul – a name applied to several
blocks, that get their effect from a counter-change of adjacent
colours. A popular name for it now is Dolly Madison's Workbox.
Dolly Madison was the young wife of James Madison, who
became president in 1808. She livened up the White House with
lavish spending on décor and social events. She has also given
her name to another block, Dolly Madison's Star.

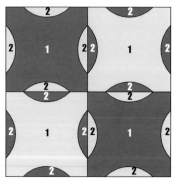
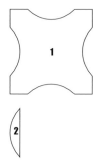

Harvest Sun

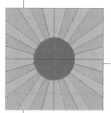

This block is taken from a quilt illustrated by Jonathan Holstein in his book *The Pieced Quilt; an American Design Tradition* (1973). He describes it as an Art Deco fan quilt; the original is entirely pieced in scrap fabrics. To draft the block, draw a square the size you want the finished block to be. Mark two sides of the square at regular intervals. Draw a line from the opposite corner to each of the marks. Use a compass to draw the arc. You'll see that for this block five templates are needed, four for the 'rays' and one for the arc. The templates on either side of the central patch must be reversed.

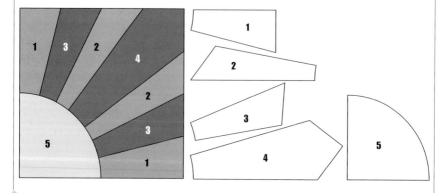

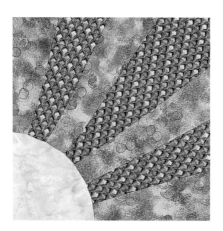

Grandmother's Fan

Ruby McKim illustrates this block as Grandmother's Fan in *101 Patchwork Designs* (1938), although the *Kansas City Star* had previously published it as Fan Quilt Block in 1935. There are several similar blocks called Grandmother's Fan but this seems to be the one most often found under that name today. As with many fan blocks, you can either piece this completely or make it by just piecing the eight segments of the fan, then appliquéing them onto a background square.

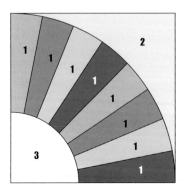

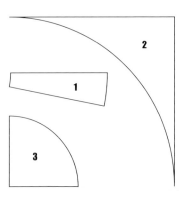

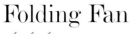

Folding Fan

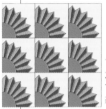

.Straight set

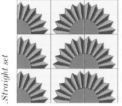

Fans flipped horizontally

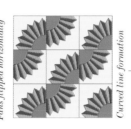

Curved line formation

The fan blades in this block give the illusion that they can be folded up like a real fan. The only published block that I can trace which resembles it is called Fancy Fan, published in the 1960s by the magazine *Aunt Kate's Quilting Bee*. The construction is not as complicated as it may look. Only one template is needed for the blades, but you must remember to use it one side up for all the dark patches, and then reverse it for all the light ones. Piece the fan first, and then stitch it onto a background square.

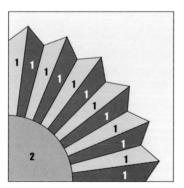

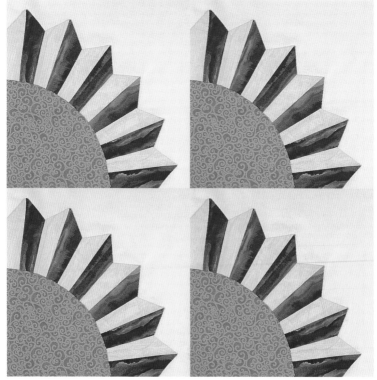

Banded Fan

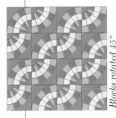

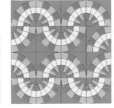

Blocks rotated 45°

Blocks rotated 90°

There are countless variations on the Fans theme and you can have fun making up your own as well. In this version, the plain central band gives a strong graphic effect whichever way you arrange the blocks.

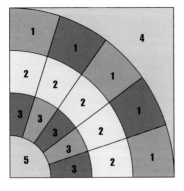

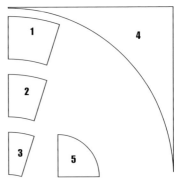

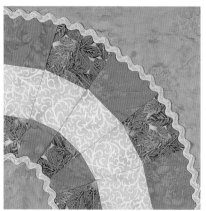

Snake Trail

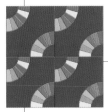

Here's a version of the traditional fan block in which two fans are placed opposite each other in a single block. This appears to be a modern interpretation of the fan, since most examples of it seem to have been published in the 1970s. The earliest sighting of it in publication is in the 1930s, and it is attributed to Nancy Cabot, who called it Rattlesnake.

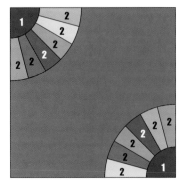

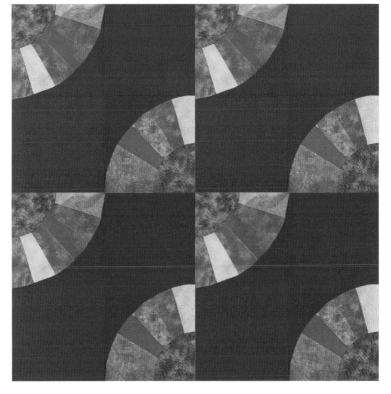

Log Cabin Basic Block

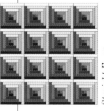

Straight Furrow

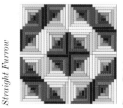

Barn Raising

Streak o' Lightning

The basic Log Cabin block doesn't need any templates. Just work around the central square alternately adding strips of dark fabric on two adjacent sides of the block and light on the other two, cutting off each strip to the required length as you go. If you start with a 5cm (2-inch) square, for example, your first strip will be 5cm (2 inches) long, the next 10cm (4 inches) and so on. But it's not necessary to measure them in advance. Just cut up lots of strips of the same width, for example 4cm (1½ inches), in dark and light fabrics.

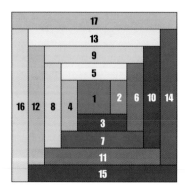

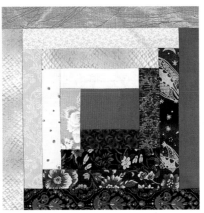

Courthouse Steps

Courthouse Steps is an easy variation of the basic Log Cabin block. Dark and light fabrics are placed on opposite sides of the square, instead of at right angles to each other as in the basic Log Cabin. Although it's a very popular block, there seems to be little evidence of it having been published in its own right. Carrie Hall, for example, illustrates it as one of several Log Cabin variations in *The Romance of the Patchwork Quilt in America* (1935). There are, however, many surviving quilts in the pattern. Averil Colby, in *Patchwork* (1958), illustrates a coverlet in rich velvet fabrics dating from around 1880, which she names simply 'Log Cabin'.

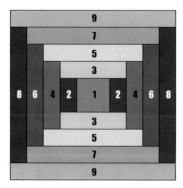

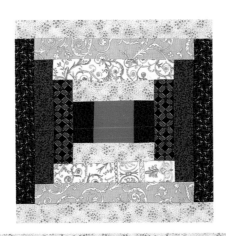

Pineapple

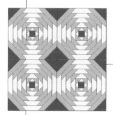

The Ladies' Art Company published this Log Cabin variation
in 1898 but, like Courthouse Steps, there seems to be little
evidence of it being published elsewhere. It is quite challenging
to make and is definitely one to piece by hand. However,
patterns can be bought for making the block on a marked
foundation, and special rulers are also available to make the
cutting easier. This pattern has gained considerable popularity
in modern times, perhaps because the availability of quilters'
tools and gadgets have made it easier to piece by machine.

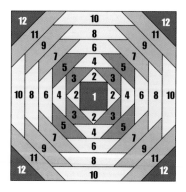

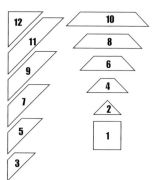

Oak Leaf and Cherries

Oak leaves are traditionally popular appliqué motifs, although it's not always possible to give a precise date for the first publication of some of these old blocks. Both Carrie Hall and Ruth Finley illustrate this one, so it's clearly a very old favourite. It also features in Dolores Hinson's *A Quilter's Companion* (1973). The appliqué patches for 'cross-over' blocks like this can be accurately aligned if you fold and press the background fabric with a hot iron to make creases and use them as a guide.

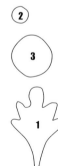

Baltimore Block

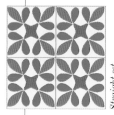

Straight set

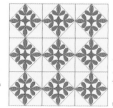

On point set

During the mid-nineteenth century, a characteristic style of appliqué quilt developed in Baltimore, USA. Since there were many people of German extraction in that community, it is generally thought that German folk art was an influence on the designs used. The blocks are often elaborate: here I've chosen one of the simpler versions, suitable for trying out the style while still achieving the authentic 'Baltimore' look. If you make the pattern on a fairly large scale, this block makes a very effective quilt, especially if you set the blocks 'on point' with a contrasting fabric for the alternating blocks.

Fleur de Lys

Another traditional Baltimore block, the Fleur de Lys is a design taken originally from heraldry. It was the armorial device of the kings of France and represents three stylised lilies. The pattern for the block is cut from a single piece of fabric, which can be cut out accurately by folding the fabric into quarters. Then trace one quarter of the pattern, as shown in the diagram, onto the fabric and cut out through all four layers at once. Open out and pin the shape to your background fabric.

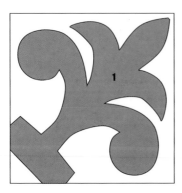

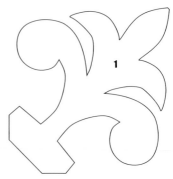

Tulip Time

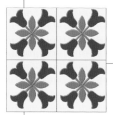

When tulips were first introduced into Europe from the East toward the end of the seventeenth century, they caused enormous excitement, amounting to tulip mania! The tulip motif has remained a favourite ever since, as popular with artists and craftsmen as with quilt makers. There are several lovely tulip patterns for appliqué or you can make up one of your own, as I have done.

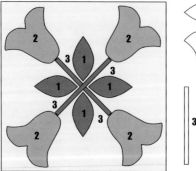

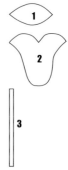

Dresden Plate

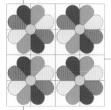

There are several versions of Dresden Plate, which is closely related to the Fan blocks (see pages 220–229) and can have any number of segments – from this eight-piece version to others with as many as sixteen segments. This block is one from the 1930s and it is quite easy to create by appliqué or by a combination of piecing and appliqué. I've used fusible webbing to apply the segments to the background, then embellished the seams with a machine embroidery stitch. Complete the block by appliquéing the centre circle.

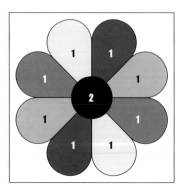

Hickory Leaf

This pattern was first published by the Ladies' Art Company in 1898 and has been published many times as a pieced block. It has also appeared under many names, including Orange Peel, Orange Slices and Irish Chain. *Country Life* magazine published it in 1923 as Job's Patience, a name which seems particularly appropriate since piecing it would certainly challenge most people's patience! I've adapted it for appliqué and recommend using the fusible webbing method to create it.

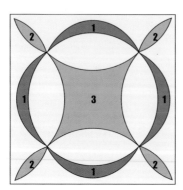

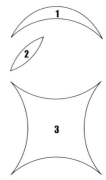

Where to go from here

One of the joys of quilting is the potential for real creativity once you've mastered the basic techniques. The possibilities are endless. The following section gives you some pointers for ways in which you may develop and establish your own style. You should use this only as a starting point, however, and not be afraid to experiment with colour, fabrics and design.

Many quiltmakers enjoy reproducing traditional blocks and even whole quilts. Several fabric manufacturers produce wonderful ranges of reproduction fabrics based on surviving quilts from the nineteenth century and making a copy of an old quilt is one way of upholding the old quiltmaking traditions and also of honouring the spirit of the original maker.

On the other hand, many contemporary quiltmakers delight in developing the tradition along their own lines so if this is where your talents and interests lie you'll find plenty of ways of developing them. Ever since the 1970s, when quilts began to come off beds and to be shown on walls as works of art, quilt art has flourished and grown in popularity so if your interests lead you in that direction we'll give you some pointers for progressing along that route.

Today I use a quilting program as a tool in designing quilts and it's certainly a great asset. But you don't NEED such a program, or even to have the first idea about using a computer. Access to a photocopier is useful since with that you can quickly photocopy outlines of blocks and use them for repeats, rotation and colourways, as explained on page 25.

▲ *Fabrics reproduced from an 1830s quilt*

Designing with blocks

There are no limits to what you can achieve when you start playing with blocks. Here are a few ideas to get you started.

Surprising effects can be achieved simply by adapting, re-colouring or re-sizing an existing block. One of my favourite ways of giving an old block a new look is to change round some or all of the units within it. That's how I came up with my Nifty Nine-Patch (see page 140), which turned out to be even more versatile than I at first thought.

▼ Double Squares

Changing the colourways in a block can also have a dramatic effect.

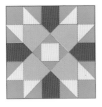

▲ Providence Block

▾ *Compass Kaleidoscope with elongated version*

Blocks don't have to be square. See what happens if you take a square block and turn it into a rectangle. To do this, simply draw a grid in which the units are all longer than they are wide and fit the units into the grid.

Give the block a setting. Refer to page 34 for different types of settings and experiment with placing the block in other settings as well. Tumbling Blocks and Boxes work well.

▸ *Blazing Star in Boxes (left) and Blazing Star in Tumbling Blocks (right)*

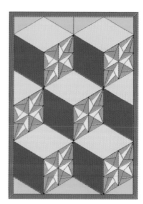

Even a plain block can be transformed by setting it with pieced sashings.

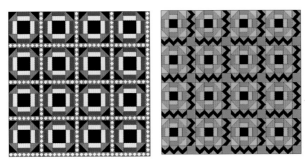

◄ *Pieced sashings*

Try combining two blocks in the same quilt. Combining piecing with appliqué has been a favourite technique since the early days of quiltmaking. You can either alternate pieced blocks with appliqué blocks, or appliqué onto pieced blocks or the borders.

Getting inspiration

Once you've mastered quiltmaking with blocks, you may want to break into a freer style of quilt design. One of the finest ways to get ideas is to visit as many quilting exhibitions as possible – especially the smaller shows held by individual guilds which often reveal unexpected quilting talent. You might also consider taking some classes with quilt teachers or artists whose methods and ideas you admire. Read as much quilting literature as you can – if you decide you want to develop a specialty in any particular field, there are bound to be books to help you on your way.

▲ *Quilt combining Eight-pointed Star with Kaleidoscope blocks.*

Remember, quiltmaking is an ever-evolving activity and one which increasingly pushes the boundaries between craft and fine art. Every contemporary quiltmaker, from humble beginner to textile artist, makes her/his contribution to its heritage – and you can do so too.

Further reading

ALBERS Josef *Interaction of Color* Yale University Press, New Haven 1971. A classic text on colour theory.

BEYER Jinny *The Quilter's Album of Blocks and Borders* EPM Publications Inc., VA 1980. Comprehensive information and instruction on drafting blocks and making templates.

BRACKMAN Barbara *Encyclopedia of Pieced Quilt Patterns* American Quilters' Society, Paducah, KY 1989. Over 4,000 block patterns identified and categorised according to their geometrical and design properties.

FISHER L. *Quilts of Illusion* Blandford, London 1990. The extraordinary optical effect of many traditional patterns explained and illustrated, includes patterns and templates to make some of them.

HARER, Michele *The Essential Guide to Practically Perfect Patchwork* Krause Publications, 2002. Starts with the basics of quilting and expands to more advanced concepts. Each of the 10 lessons builds on the previous. A good foundation book.

HOLSTEIN J. *The Pieced Quilt; an American Design Tradition* New York Graphic Society 1973. The definitive account of the history, traditions and significance of the American patchwork quilt. The author is credited with the 1970s revival of interest in quilts and quilt making as both art and craft, which led to the contemporary 'boom'.

JAMES M. *The Quiltmaker's Handbook* Prentice-Hall, US 1978.
After twenty years, still one of the best and most comprehensive guides to design, technique and colour, with very thorough and detailed 'how-to' instructions. Includes designing and drafting your own blocks and making and using templates.

KHIN Yvonne M. *The Collector's Dictionary of Quilt Names and Patterns* Acropolis Books Ltd., Washington DC 1980. 2,400 quilt blocks illustrated and described by category and name.

MALONE Maggie *1001 Patchwork Designs* Sterling Publishing Co. Inc., NY 1982. Every block shown with construction lines and shading. Indispensable.

SPECKMAN D. *Pattern Play* C & T Publishing, US 1993.
An innovative approach to quilt design and technique. Includes ways of adapting traditional blocks or creating your own and using them in quilts. Also, very detailed and easy to follow instructions and tips to achieve accurate piecing.

Index

A
Air Castle 150
American block piecing 28–30
Amish Style 194
appliqué 33
Art Square 196
assembly 36
Attic Windows 76
Aunt Sukey's Choice 164
B
Balkan Puzzle 68
Baltimore Block 238
Banded Fan 226
Barbara Fitchie Star 66
Blazing Star 180
Bleeding Hearts 206
borders 35
Bow Tie 64
Brick Wall 48
Broken Band 204
Bull's Eye 114
C
Card Trick 154
Cat's Cradle 134
Celia's Nifty Nine-Patch 140
Celia's Pinwheel Square 104
Chevron 52
Church Window 58
Churn Dash 132
Clay's Choice 72
Columbia, The 192
Corn and Beans 198
Country Roads 120
Courthouse Steps 232
Cross and Crown 100
D
Diamond Star 94
Dogtooth Violet 88
Double Pinwheel 82
Double Squares 200
Dove in the Window 130
Dresden Plate 244
Drunkard's Path 212
E
Eccentric Star 166
English patchwork 31

F
Fifty-four–Forty or Fight 160
Fleur de Lys 240
Folding Fan 224
foundation piecing 32
Four-Patch Weave 84
frames 19
Friendship Star 168
G
Georgia 112
Grandmother's Choice 96
Grandmother's Fan 222
Grandmother's Flower Garden 50
Greek Cross 122
Guiding Star 170
H
Harvest Sun 220
Hickory Leaf 246
hoops 19
I
Indian Arrowhead 74
J
Jack in the Box 102
Jacob's Ladder 146
K
Kaleidoscope 186
Kentucky Chain 78
Key West Beauty 92
L
Lady of the Lake 106
layouts 34
Little Rock Block 152
Lincoln's Platform 124
Log Cabin Basic Block 230
M
Melon Patch 208
Minnesota 98
Miss Jackson 190
Morning Star 174
N
Nelson's Victory 62
Nifty Star 172
Night and Day 70
Nine-Patch Frame 138
1904 Star 182
Nocturne 216

North Carolina Lily 128
Northumberland Star 90
O
Oak Leaf and Cherries 236
Ohio Star 148
P
Peter and Paul 218
Pine Tree 108
Pineapple 234
Prairie Flower 156
Prosperity Block 158
Providence Block 110
Q
quilting 37–9
R
Rail Fence 54
Ribbon Quilt Block 136
Road to Paradise, The 144
Rosebud 126
S
sashings 36
Shaded Nine-Patch 142
Six-sided Star 188
Snake Trail 228
Spider Web 184
Star of Le Moyne 176
Storm at Sea 86
Streak o' Lightning 56
Swing in the Center 162
T
thread 18
Tobacco Leaf 210
Trailing Star 80
Tulip Time 242
Tumbling Blocks 60
Turkey Tracks 116
V
Virginia Reel 202
Virginia Star 178
W
wadding 17
Walls of Jericho 118
Winding Ways 214

254

Suppliers

Becky Sharp's Quilting
7 Eversliegh Drive
Bebington
Wirral
CH63 3DD
Tel/Fax: 0151 201 3643
Web: www.becky-sharps-quilting.com

Creations Direct
Mail Order Dept.
1 Denecroft Gardens
Grays
Essex
RM17 5SA
Tel: 0870 745220
Fax: 0870 7425221
Web: www.creativedirect.co.uk

Creative Quilting
3 Bridge Road
East Moleset
Surrey
KT8 9EU
Tel: 020 8941 7075
Fax: 020 8979 3381
Web:
www.creativequilting.co.uk

Dreamcatcher Quilts
5a Beulah Road
Rhiwbina
Cardiff
Tel: 029 2069 4666
Web: dreamcatcherquilts.co.uk

Fun 2 Do
7a Oliver Place,
Hawick,
Roxburghshire,
TD9 9BG
Tel/Fax: 01450 370103
www.fun2do.co.uk

House of Patchwork
Unit 18/19 Tower Centre
Hoddesdon
Herts
EN11 8UB
Tel: 01992 447544
Fax: 01992 446892
Web:
www.houseofpatchwork.co.uk

Just Sew
Poet's Walk
Penrith
Cumbria
CA11 7HJ
Tel: 01768 866791

Patchwork Plus
129 Station Road
Cark
Grange over Sands
Cumbria
LA11 7NY
Tel: 01539 559009
Fax: 01539 559009
Web:
www.patchworkplus.co.uk

Pauline's Patchwork
Brewer's Quay
Hope Square
Weymouth
Dorset
DT4 8TR
Tel: 01305 766543
Web:
www.paulinespatchwork.co.uk

The Patchwork Gallery
17 Mead Close
Knutsford
Cheshire, WA16 0DU
Tel: 01565 632 553
Web:
www.home.btclick.com/patch workgallery

Patchwork Direct
Wesleyan House
Dale Road North
Darley Dale
Derbyshire
DE4 2HX
Tel: 01629 734100
Fax: 01629 734100
Web:www.patchworkdirect.com

The Quilt Room
20 West Street
Dorking
Surrey
RH4 1BL
Tel: 01306 877307
Fax: 01306 877407
Web: www.quiltroom.co.uk

Rio Designs (Computer
software for quilters)
Flint Cottage
]Treacle Lane
Rushden
Buntingford
Herts
SG9 0SL
Tel/Fax: 01763 288234
Web: www.riodesigns.co.uk

Stitch in Time
293 Sandycombe Road
Kew
Surrey
TW9 3LU
Tel: 020 8948 8462
Fax: 020 8948 8462
Web: www.stitchintime.co.uk

Australia

Bay Fabric & Patchwork
Shop 5, Blandford Plaza
2 Orient Street
Batemans Bay
New South Wales 2536
Tel: (02) 4472 9808
Fax: (02) 4472 3779

Patches of Heaven
173 Hoskins Street
Tremora
New South Wales
Tel: (02) 6978 1133

Patchwork by Sea
49 Jetty Road
Brighton
South Australia 5048
Tel: +61 8377 3942
Web:
www.patchworkbysea.com.au

North America

Clover Needlecraft, Inc
1007 E Dominguez St #L
Carson, CA 90746
Tel: 310-516-7846

Colonial Needle Co
74 Westmoreland Ave
White Plains, NY 10606
Tel: 914-946-7474
Web: www.colonialneedle.com

EZ Quilting by Wrights
85 South St
West Warren, MA 01092
Tel: 800-628-9362
Web: www.ezquilt.com

Credits

Author acknowledgements:
Grateful thanks to the following quilting friends for help and support: Christine Gash for
help with blocks and advice on fabrics and colours and Carolyn Madden for being the
"hands" in all the photography as well as contributing lots of sensible advice.

Pat Swainson of Just Sew, Penrith, kindly lent equipment and fabrics.

Quarto would like to thank and acknowledge the following for permission to reproduce
pictures:
p. 8   1718 silk patchwork © The Quilters' Guild of the British Isles
p. 9   Medallion quilt, reproduced by permission of the American Museum in Bath, Britain.

All other photographs and illustrations are the copyright of Quarto.

Fabrics on p. 240 were produced by Makower UK for The Quilters' Guild of the British
Isles.

While every effort has been made to credit contributors, Quarto would like to apologise
should there have been any omissions or errors.